THE **PRINCETON** REVIEW

CRACKING THE SYSTEM

THE LSAT

1992 EDITION

THE **PRINCETON** REVIEW

CRACKING THE SYSTEM

THE LSAT

1992 EDITION

BY ADAM ROBINSON
AND THE STAFF OF
THE PRINCETON REVIEW

VILLARD BOOKS NEW YORK 1991

Library of Congress Cataloging-in-Publication Data
Robinson, Adam
   The Princeton Review—1992 Edition—The LSAT:
Cracking the System.

   At head of title: The Princeton Review.
   1. Law schools—United States—Entrance examinations.
I. Robinson, Adam.   II. Princeton Review (Firm)
III. Title   IV. Title: Princeton Review: Cracking the System.
KF285.Z9R6   1991   340'.076   87-19010
ISBN 0-679-73139-3

Manufactured in the United States of America

9 8 7 6 5 4 3 2

Revised Edition

DESIGNED BY BARBARA MARKS

FOREWORD

Summary of Changes in the New LSAT

Well, the LSAT psychometricians have been tinkering with the LSAT once again. Not to worry. The changes are significant, but not momentous. Actually, we have to take our hats off to the test writers—the new LSAT *is* actually a better test.

Since many students are familiar with the previous format of the LSAT, we will summarize the changes now.

1. The LSAT has become *much* more competitive. Since Wall Street's crash of '87, tens of thousands of would-be investment bankers have discovered consciences and become would-be lawyers. Apparently, this skewed the "curve." Too many students achieved inflated LSAT scores. To restore the proper score distribution, **the very hardest questions on the LSAT will now be even harder.** This may be small comfort, but the very easiest questions on the LSAT will also be easier.

   The upshot? It just got harder to slam-dunk the LSAT, but the free-throw line moved a few feet closer to the hoop. Expect fewer people to score in the highest and lowest score ranges.

2. LSAT scores now range from 120 to 180, instead of the old 10 to 48. (Drop the initial one and add a zero at the end and voilá—the new scale becomes the familiar 200 to 800 scale.)

3. **We now have strong reason to believe that the questions in each section will approximate some rough order of difficulty.** That is, the first reading passage will probably be easier than the last passage; the first game will probably be easier than the last.

   The questions within a passage or a game set, however, probably will *not* be arranged in order of difficulty. The first question on a particular passage could be easier or harder than the last question on that passage.

4. Instead of three 45-minute sections that count (Reading Passages, Arguments, and Games), the LSAT now has four 35-minute sections (Reading Passages, *two* Arguments, and Games).

5. **Arguments are now the most heavily weighted question type;** more than twice as important as Games, the most feared question type.

6. The passages in the Reading section are now drawn almost entirely from law review articles. They are much better written than the murky passages of old.

7. Curiously, although the wording of the reading passages has become more clear, the wording of reading *questions* has become more slippery. A question that seems to be straightforward and refer to explicit passage statements, for examples, might actually require inferential thinking—going beyond what the passage says to what it *implies*.

   Another warning: Format questions that used to highlight key words like NOT ("Which of the following issues is NOT addressed by the author?") now sometimes leave those words in lowercase. Read questions *carefully*.

8. Ditto with the wording of Arguments questions. Watch your step.

9. The Games are noticeably easier and less convoluted than they were a couple of years ago. As we noted though, the hardest games just got harder. Still, the Games section now contributes only 23% of your score (down from 30%). Don't obsess over this section unless it's your only weak point.

10. There now seems to be a slight but exploitable pattern to answers. For the 99% of test takers who do not have time to answer every question, we can lift your odds of blind guessing from 20% to 25% or more. Every little bit helps.

We will expand on each of these points in the chapters to follow.

FOREWORD
TO THE FIRST EDITION

Why This Book Took over Two Years to Publish

In early September 1986, the first book in this series was published. *Cracking the System:* The SAT received instant acclaim that was soon to place it on the best-seller lists. A week after its publication, we made a trip down to New Hope, Pennsylvania, headquarters of the Law School Admissions Council/Law School Admissions Services. We had been working for some time on what was to be the third *Cracking the System* title, this one on the LSAT. We were puzzled by the lack of certain statistical information on the LSAT that was publicly available on all the other standardized admissions tests. We needed this information and we also wanted to inform the LSAC/LSAS that we were working on an LSAT book.

We spoke with one representative of LSAC/LSAS who was polite but not particularly forthcoming with statistical information that we requested. Again, this information is routinely provided on other tests like the SAT, GRE, GMAT, and even the MCAT. Frustrated, we were just about to leave when one of the principal executives of LSAC/LSAS introduced himself. He had just seen the rave review of our SAT book in *The Wall Street Journal.*

Far from maintaining a bureaucratic reserve, he embraced us enthusiastically. Not only did he promise the support of the LSAC/LSAS, he even proposed the possibility of various joint ventures.

We were astonished, but not about to look this gift horse in the mouth. If the LSAC/LSAS wanted to work together with The Princeton Review, great! We made two other trips to New Hope to meet with this executive. At all of these meetings he pledged his support of our undertaking and continued to suggest possible joint ventures.

Thinking we had the complete cooperation of the LSAC/LSAS, we set about finishing the LSAT book, turning in the finished manuscript during the late spring of 1987.

Now, one of the perfunctory matters in submitting the manuscript was securing copyright permission from the LSAC/LSAS. As in our SAT book, our LSAT book included numerous examples from actual LSATs. With our SAT book, this was no problem. All we had to do was pay a nominal licensing fee to the Educational Testing Service, an organization with which we were actually engaged in a sizable legal dispute. It should be no problem securing copyright permission from the LSAC/LSAS. After all, they even wanted to do joint ventures with us! Wrong.

Our encouraging executive contact was no longer with the LSAC/LSAS and our original contact sat on our request for two months despite phone calls from us and our publisher. Finally, they gave us their answer. We could not reprint the questions in any form.

After many months, they finally agreed to allow us to reprint an entire LSAT, but only in its entirety, making it difficult and awkward to analyze any of the individual questions. What good would that have done students?

At great expense and with still further delays, we decided to rewrite the book using our own illustrative questions. We shaped these questions to reflect both the variety and difficulty of actual LSAT questions.

The LSAC/LSAS refusal to grant copyright permission raised numerous legal issues, foremost among them being the doctrine of "fair use." Our publisher, however, chose not to challenge the LSAC/LSAS. We tried for over two years to include actual LSAT questions. We finally relented when we realized that students would be better off with a book of our techniques, even if we couldn't illustrate them on real questions. We gave it our best shot. Perhaps you students should lobby for reasonable (i.e., cheap) access to LSAT questions with commentary by some organization other than the LSAC/LSAS.

ACKNOWLEDGMENTS

A successful LSAT program is a collaborative effort. We'd especially like to thank our teachers John Sheehan, Lindsey van Wagenen, Mark Sawula, Jim Reynolds, Adam Frank, and Adam Landis for their suggestions and contributions. Special thanks are owed John Hasnas.

We'd like to thank our agent, Julia Coopersmith, for her tireless help and editorial suggestions. To our editor Diane Reverand, our deep appreciation for her patience with our perfectionist delays and for her sponsorship of the entire *Cracking the System* project. And many thanks to Emily Bestler, now associate editor at Villard, and Martha Schueneman, Diane's able assistant—we realize authors aren't always easy to deal with.

A very special thanks to Oliver Hart, professor of economics at M.I.T., and to Debora Davies and the folks at Columbia Law Review for their generous permission to quote an excerpt from an article by Professor Hart.

Finally, we'd like to thank all those who have taught us everything we know about taking tests—our students.

CONTENTS

THE **PRINCETON** REVIEW

CRACKING THE SYSTEM

THE LSAT

1992 EDITION

CHAPTER 1

Orientation: How to Think About the LSAT

What is the Law School Admission Test?

The Law School Admission Test (LSAT) is a three-and-one-half hour multiple-choice test divided into five sections:

1. a 27-question Reading Passages section
2. two 25-question Arguments sections
3. a 23-question Games section
4. an Experimental section

The number of questions may vary slightly from those just indicated, but the total number of questions on your test will fall somewhere between 96 and 104.

Each of these sections lasts 35 minutes. The order of the sections in your test booklet will almost certainly differ from the order given above. You may have seen these sections referred to by names different from the ones we have given them. The sections have no official names; they will not be labeled in your test booklet.

The Experimental section does not count toward your LSAT score. An experimental section may look like any of the four genuine sections. The publisher of the LSAT uses this section to try out new questions and to gauge the difficulty of your LSAT in relation to that of past LSATs.

The Sixth Section of the LSAT

In addition to spending 35 minutes doing unpaid research and development work for the LSAT publishers, you will also have to spend 30 minutes writing an essay that no one will ever read and that will not count toward your LSAT score. We'll tell you everything you need to know about this essay, called the Writing Sample, in Chapter 6.

When is the LSAT Given?

The LSAT is given four times a year: February, June, October, and December. Application deadlines are strict and are made weeks in advance. **Sign up as early as possible.**

Where Does the LSAT Come From?

The LSAT is written under the supervision of the Law School Admissions Services (LSAS), which is the operational arm of the Law School Admissions Council (LSAC). LSAC is an association of American and Canadian law schools. It is the law school equivalent of the College Board.

What Does the LSAT Test?

The LSAT is an arbitrary obstacle placed between you and the profession you hope to enter. You have no choice but to take it. All the nation's accredited law schools require it.

The LSAT is a test of how good you are at taking the LSAT. It is not a test of anything that lawyers do, or even of anything that law students do. The LSAC/LSAS psychometricians will pull out statistical tables pointing to this correlation and that correlation. To the extent that the LSAT correlates with the grades of a law school, we would question that school's grading system.

Law school exams are primarily essay tests. Not so the LSAT, where the essay does not affect your score. Moreover, while legal thinking may appear to arrive at inevitable answers to complex questions through the application of immutable principles and inexorable logic, there is, in fact, no "best" answer to most legal questions. Indeed, legal thinking is the paradigm of dialectical reasoning. Not on the LSAT, which rewards the ability to select the pat answer deemed "best" by a committee of test writers. Anyone able to see the merit of other positions (the incorrect answer choices) is going to have a lot of trouble on the LSAT.

If you took the SAT in high school, you probably have a pretty good idea of how well you'll do on the LSAT. The LSAT, however, is *much* more difficult than the SAT. Even students who scored very well on the SAT should prepare for the LSAT.

Why Did They Change the LSAT Again?

Because this test is a turkey. The LSAC/LSAS loves tinkering with it. Every couple of years their research department unveils a *new! improved!* LSAT.

All ribbing aside, we have to admit that the latest LSAT, while far from perfect, is a laudable advancement over the previous fiascoes.

How Is the LSAT Scored?

Four or five weeks after you take the LSAT, you will receive a report from the LSAS with copies of your LSAT, your responses, the answer key, and your score.

The new scale of LSAT scores ranges from 120 to 180. A score of 180 is considered perfect, but you don't have to answer every question correctly to earn this score (something only one LSAT taker in a thousand achieves). Depending on the difficulty of the particular test you take, you could miss anywhere from four to eight questions and still earn a "perfect" score. After that, every three missed questions will cost you two points.

LSAT Scores and Percentiles

Along with your LSAT score, you will receive a percentile ranking. This ranking compares your performance with that of everyone else who has taken the LSAT for the previous five years. Since 150 is the average LSAT score, it would receive a percentile ranking of 50. A score of 155 moves up to a ranking of 70. A 160 pulls you up to a ranking of 85. And any score over 166 puts you above 95 percent of the LSAT takers.

The following table summarizes how many mistakes you can make on one hundred questions and still reach your LSAT goal. Notice that 90 percent of those taking the test make more than twenty-three errors. Remember that when you think you should try to finish each and every question. **This table estimates the scoring on the new version of the LSAT on the basis of the scales used on the old version.**

Approximate Number of Errors (out of 100)	New LSAT Score	Percentile Rank	Old LSAT Score	200–800 Equivalent
4	180	99 + +%	48	800
10	175	99 +	46	750
16	170	97 +	43	700
22	165	93 +	40	650
28	160	84 +	37	600
34	155	69 +	34	550
40	150	50 +	31	500
46	145	31 +	27	450
52	140	15 +	22	400
58	135	6 +	17	350

The last two columns are provided for comparison purposes.

When interpreting your percentile rank, keep in mind that you are competing against sophisticated test takers. A score of 150, for example, means that you are an average tester among a crowd of some very strong test takers.

How Accurate Are LSAT Scores?

About as accurate as those of any other multiple-choice, standardized test. Which is to say, not nearly so accurate as the LSAC would have you believe. Can you believe that the LSAC psychometricians use a formula supposedly accurate to six decimal places! Give us a break. Don't let such pseudoscientific accuracy deceive you.

How Much Weight Are LSAT Scores Given?

A lot.

It varies from school to school, but the bottom line is that your LSAT score is *crucial*. **Some law schools weigh your LSAT score twice as much as your grades.**

The law school admissions process is mechanical: If you have good grades and a good LSAT score, you get in; if you don't, you don't. Most law schools do not conduct interviews. Most don't even have a full-time admissions staff.

You might think that law schools should consider more than grades and LSAT scores. In some cases they do, but most of the time they don't. The vast majority of admissions decisions are made in just a few seconds.

What About My Grades?

Most of the law schools to which you apply will learn about your grades from the Law School Data Assembly Service (LSDAS). This outfit reduces the type and the difficulty of the courses you've taken and your grades to a single number: the GPA. The message is clear: Get the highest GPA possible.

This GPA, your LSAT score, and some other pieces of information are then summarized on a single piece of paper so that part-time law school admissions officers can decide your fate more quickly than they would be able to if they had to look at several pieces of paper.

LSDAS made some colossal screwups in the days when it was run by ETS. We know of one instance, for example, where a student's A − average was reported to law schools by LSDAS as a C +, with predictable consequences for the applicant. (Whoops!) **It may be better run now, but you should still make absolutely certain that the information about you that it sends out to the law schools is correct.**

How You Can Improve Your Admissions Chances

It's almost certainly too late to do anything about your grades, but you can give your LSAT score a big boost if you put your mind to it. Since the LSAT score is given such enormous weight in law school admissions decisions, time spent preparing for the test can have a big payoff.

When you should start preparing depends on your schedule, your test-taking skills, and the score you hope to achieve. Roughly speaking, you can expect to spend a week for every point you hope to add to your score.

Make no mistake about it: **The LSAT is no piece of cake.** Of all the standardized tests, the LSAT is one of the most difficult. It is certainly more difficult than the SAT you took over four years ago. Improving your LSAT score won't be easy. We have tried to make it as much fun as possible, but brace yourself for some heavy going.

How You Will Improve Your LSAT Score

The LSAT is a tough test, but as with any other test, you can improve your score with smart preparation. Our techniques will help you raise your LSAT score by teaching you to

1. think like the LSAT writers
2. take full advantage of the limited time allowed
3. find the answers to questions you do not understand
4. avoid the traps LSAT writers set for you; indeed you will use these traps to your own advantage
5. raise your score by spending time on fewer questions

Practice, Practice, Practice

This book can give you a big advantage. The Princeton Review has analyzed every LSAT that has ever been made public, and we've honed our techniques on thousands of students. Our techniques work because they are derived from real LSATs.

In addition to studying this book, you need to get your hands on and study as many real LSATs as you can. The more recent the test, the better (but avoid the quirky tests from February 1986 to March 1989).

The ideal practice materials are released LSAT disclosure booklets. Although previous LSATs have different section formats from those on the new LSAT, the individual questions are virtually indistinguishable. You can receive an LSAT order form of available LSATs by writing to

LSAC/LSAS
P.O. Box 2000
Newtown, PA 18940-0998

Do it today. If you're in a rush, their number is (215) 968-1001.

LSAC/LSAS also publishes a number of books that you may find helpful:

The Official Guide to U.S. Law Schools (The Prelaw Handbook)
This book lists law school data, including statistical charts that allow you to match up your GPA and LSAT score against those of the applicants admitted to any particular school. You learn, for example, that a certain well-known competitive law school admits 70 percent of the applicants with a 40+ LSAT score and 3.75+ GPA, but only 50 percent of those with LSAT scores and GPAs just a notch below these. You should keep in mind that these tables reflect the school averages and may or may not include "Special Admissions."

Financing Your Law School Education
This book is a guide to all the legal ways of finding and getting your hands on the tens of thousands of dollars the next three years are going to cost. By the way, the LSAC/LSAS coordinates *Law Access: A National Loan Program for Legal Education.* Ask for this packet, which contains information on getting an education loan.

The Right Law School for You
This book tells you what to look for beyond "reputation" in choosing a law school, and includes useful information on how to get in.

The official LSAT PrepKit contains workbooks and is probably worth getting, but forget their funky PrepWare™ software. While these books contain useful information about the way test writers think, you should ignore

any test-taking "techniques" or advice, much of which is trite, if not dubious.

I Thought the Law School Admission Service Was "Nonprofit." Why Do They Charge So Much Money for Their Services?

Can you spell *m-o-n-o-p-o-l-y* or *b-u-r-e-a-u-c-r-a-t-i-c w-a-s-t-e?*

Most applicants to graduate school take their admissions tests once. Assuming that you will also buy a guidebook and a few practice exams, here is a list comparing the various costs:

GRE	$ 36.00
GMAT	$ 45.90
MCAT	$ 75.50
LSAT	$104.00

But wait, there's more! Most law schools require you to subscribe to the LSDAS, which is going to set you back more money. **If you have any special requests or want other publications, you could be looking at two hundred dollars or more.**

Taking the LSAT is more than twice as expensive as taking either the GRE or the GMAT. The LSAC/LSAS might argue that it has fewer applicants taking the LSAT than either of those tests, over which it must distribute its overhead. But the LSAT still costs a lot more than the MCAT, which has far fewer applicants.

By the most conservative estimate, the LSAC/LSAS is pulling in $15,000,000 to $20,000,000 a year. Nonprofit? We heard through the grapevine that one former LSAS executive was sacked because he was scheming to take the organization private.

Maybe you can explain it to us.

A Warning

Many of our LSAT techniques violate cherished test-taking myths you may have heard over the years. Some of our techniques may even appear to violate what you think of as common sense. In order to get the full benefit of our techniques, you must *trust* them. The best way to develop this trust is to practice the technique and convince yourself that they work.

When you practice, you must use real LSATs. If you try our technique on the simulated LSATs in the popular practice books, you will probably decide that the techniques don't work.

Why?

Because the questions in those books or courses may look like real LSAT questions, but they are in fact quite different. Studying the practice questions in these other books or courses could actually *hurt* your LSAT score. **Beware of any LSAT preparation book or course that uses anything other than actual released LSATs.** Even the questions in this book are not exactly the same as actual LSAT questions, although we have designed them according to the same statistical requirements used by the LSAC/LSAS. As we explain in the Foreword, we made every effort to secure copyright permission from the LSAC/LSAS, which made it virtually impossible for us to do so.

Oh, and in case we forgot to mention it, the LSAS has a monopoly on these released tests, too.

How to Use This Book

The concepts and techniques in this book have been spelled out step-by-step, building from our basic techniques to our advanced. Begin each chapter by getting an overview. Skim the headings and read the chapter summary. Then read the chapter and do the drills conscientiously.

When Should I Start Preparing?

Ideally, you should start preparing at least two months before your exam date. To get an idea of where you stand now, take an actual LSAT—*timed*. Get a friend to time you. After your *friend*—not you—scores it, decide what score you'd like to achieve. **Figure that you'll have to budget a week of active preparation for every three points you want to raise your score.**

I Just Bought This Book, But the Test Is Only a Week Away! What Should I Do?

Read Chapter 2 carefully. Read all the chapter summaries and work through the practice questions. **Almost everyone can improve his or her LSAT score simply by slowing down and working out fewer questions. Don't forget to guess on any questions you don't get to.**

If you haven't done any preparation for the LSAT, make sure you understand Arguments. Your performance on Reading Passages will improve if you familiarize yourself with how difficult they can be. Ditto with Games.

Get your hands on some actual LSATs this minute!

CHAPTER 2

Cracking
the LSAT:
Basic
Principles

You Already Know All the Answers

If someone offered to give you all the answers to the LSAT before you took it, you would probably be shocked. The fact is that every student who takes the test gets to see the answers ahead of time.

There's nothing strange or suspect about this. The LSAT is a multiple-choice test. This means that every question on it is followed by five answer choices. In every single instance, one, and only one, of these choices will be the answer. You will never have to come up with the answer entirely from scratch. All you will have to do is identify it.

How Do I Identify the Best Answer?

By focusing on the *incorrect* choices. **It is almost always easier to show why a particular choice is incorrect than to show why the answer is "best."** You will discover that on virtually all LSAT questions, the quickest way to find the answer is to find and eliminate the incorrect choices.

Process of Elimination *(POE)*

The *process of elimination,* which we call *POE,* is an extremely important concept, and one that we'll come back to again and again. It is a vital key to improving your LSAT score. By the time you finish this book, you will be able to use *POE* to answer many questions you don't fully understand.

Remember: **The basis of *POE* is focusing on incorrect choices rather than worrying about the answer.** The answer is simply the choice you can't find a valid reason to eliminate.

POE Is Also the Key to Good Guessing

Your LSAT score is based solely on the number of correct responses you make. You are not penalized for incorrect answers. A wrong answer counts the same as a space left blank—zero. **This means that you should never, never leave a blank on your answer sheet.** Guessing blindly will give you at least one chance in five of being right. Looked at another way, every seven or eight blind guesses will probably increase your LSAT score by one point. By using *POE* and our other techniques wisely, you can do much better than this.

Keep Track of Your Responses

POE will also increase your test-taking speed. Many students waste valuable time on the LSAT by rereading answer choices they have already disqualified.

To keep from doing this, cross out the choices in your booklet as you eliminate them. You paid for your test booklet; act as though you own it.

You Can't Do It in Your Head

Many students mistakenly believe that they will save time by performing calculations and doing analyses in their heads.

Don't believe it.

You're going to have enough trouble on the LSAT without depriving yourself of scratch paper. Your test booklet is your scratch paper. Use it. Cross out incorrect choices, make diagrams, and mark key points.

Transfer Your Answers in Groups

You can save up to a few minutes each section by transferring your answers from your test booklet to your answer sheet in groups. Most students work one question, find the correct spot on their answer sheet, darken it, and then return to where they left off in their test booklet. The process of going back and forth from test booklet to answer sheet consumes much too much time and invites mistakes.

Instead, circle correct answers in your booklet and wait until you finish a set of questions, or a page in the booklet, before transferring your responses to your answer sheet.

By the way, on the SAT, GRE, and GMAT no letter ever appears as the correct answer more than three times in a row. **This is not always true of the LSAT.** When you transfer your answers in groups, you may notice that you have three or even four letters in a row. Don't panic. (But see our rules for guessing at the end of each chapter.)

Any Fool Can Finish the Test—Don't!

You don't get extra credit for finishing the test early. In fact, anyone who finishes a section early is either a genius or an idiot. The LSAT is deliberately designed to prevent any student from answering every question correctly. Keep in mind that only one test taker in a thousand gets a "perfect" 180, and even that "perfect" can include as many as eight errors.

Slow down!

Raise Your Score by Working Out *Fewer* Questions!

If you think you have enough time to work out each and every question on the test, you're not working them out. Simply by ignoring the hard questions in each section, you give yourself more time to find the correct answers on questions you *can* handle.

The LSAT is what psychometricians refer to as a "highly speeded" test. That is, most students don't have time to finish it. If you push hard to work out every question, you'll make dozens of careless mistakes and decimate your score.

Ignore the hard questions and raise your score.

But Don't Forget to Guess

When we tell you to skip questions or even entire sets, we don't mean that you should fail to mark a response. Remember: **Never leave a question blank.** When we tell you to omit a question, we mean that you should simply mark a response without reading the question. **We will consider special guessing rules at the end of each section.**

Are LSAT Questions in Order of Difficulty?

On most standardized tests, the test makers arrange the questions in order of difficulty. This is true on the SAT, the GRE, the GMAT, and the MCAT. The questions in each section start off easy and then become increasingly difficult throughout the section. On such tests you can simply ignore the questions at the end of the section.

The Princeton Review has good reason to suspect that this will also be true on the new LSAT.

Still, Begin Each Section by Getting the Big Picture

Since we cannot be absolutely sure yet about whether the new LSAT will be arranged by difficulty, start each new section by getting the big picture. Check out the entire section to see which questions or sets are the most difficult; these will probably be toward the end. You will sidestep these difficult questions or sets and get to them last, if at all. **In all the sections, format questions (*Triple True/False,* and *EXCEPT/LEAST/NOT* questions) are the trickiest and most time-consuming.** We'll give you specific instructions in each chapter that will help you determine which questions of each type you should ignore.

Summary

1. Your test booklet will include the answer to every question.

2. Find the answer by eliminating the incorrect choices. Use the process of elimination (*POE*) to back into the answer.

3. Record your answers in the margin of your booklet before transferring them to your answer sheet.

4. Write all over your test booklet. You can't do everything in your head.

5. Transfer your answers to the answer sheet in blocks.

6. Do not try to finish the test unless you are absolutely confident you can score well above a 165. Otherwise you will raise your score by doing fewer questions.

7. There is no penalty for incorrect answers. Be sure to fill in answers for all questions you didn't get to work out.

8. LSAT questions in each section may be in some rough order of difficulty.

9. Begin each section by getting the big picture. The most difficult sets of problems are probably near the end, but do a quick survey to be sure. Once you've scoped out a section, budget your time accordingly.

CHAPTER 3

Reading Passages

The Reading Passages section contains four passages, varying in length from 400 to 550 words. Each passage is followed by six to eight questions. The section totals 26 to 28 questions.

Before we begin, take a moment to read the instructions to this section:

> Directions: Each passage in this section is followed by questions based on its content. After reading the passage, choose the best answer to each question and blacken the corresponding space on the answer sheet. Answer all questions following a passage on the basis of what is stated or implied in that passage.

These are the directions that will appear on your LSAT. They will not change in substance. Review them now. Don't waste time in the test room reading them. Don't even glance at them.

How You Will Improve Your Reading Score

Because you can read, and probably read well, you may think this chapter less important than the more specialized chapters. Beware: The reading passages on the LSAT are nothing like the reading material you are used to. Your reading habits have developed over many years. Although these habits have undoubtedly served you well for the most part, the passages you will encounter on the LSAT are quite different from the reading you are used to doing. Some of your reading habits might get you in deep trouble on the LSAT.

This chapter will teach you how to tailor your reading habits to fit the peculiar requirements of standardized test passages. Our techniques will enable you to

1. improve your score by working out *fewer* questions
2. read quickly and efficiently by *not* reading everything closely
3. eliminate answer choices that could not possibly be right
4. take advantage of outside knowledge
5. identify trap choices
6. find hidden answers
7. answer some questions without reading the passage

How to Read This Chapter

The best predictor of how well you'll do on LSAT reading passages is your old SAT verbal score. SAT scores and LSAT scores are very closely correlated. In fact, SAT scores are better predictors of LSAT scores than they are of college grades. If you scored above 700 on the SAT verbal section, you shouldn't have a problem with this section of the test. Even so, we can show you ways to boost your score higher.

If you were disappointed with your SAT verbal score, you need to pay very careful attention to the techniques in this chapter. No matter what your past experience, scoring higher on the Reading Passages section is a skill that can be learned. All you need to do is adjust your reading habits to fit the test.

Where Do LSAT Passages Come From?

Reading passages adapted primarily from law review articles. This doesn't mean that you have to know anything about the law to answer the questions. You don't. Ignorance of the law never hurt anyone on the LSAT.

Recent passages have stressed social-political-economic-historical-legal-ethical themes. Here are the titles of some of the articles from which they have been drawn:

Efficiency and Fairness in Insurance Risk Classification
Where Will All The Children Go: The New Kansas Preference for Joint Custody

Reporting the Facts as They Are Not Known: Media Responsibility in Concealed Human Rights Violations

These passages require no special knowledge on your part, although the economic passages appear to give an unfair advantage to students who have taken an economics course. For that reason we have chosen an economic topic as our illustrative sample later in the chapter.

The Good News

As we observed in the Foreword, reading passages on the current LSAT are an almost shocking improvement over those of previous tests.

We're not saying they're easy. The writing style is somewhat academic (the passages are law review excerpts, after all). Straightforward as they are, the passages still cover rather weighty topics. All things considered though, LSAT reading passages are now better than those of all the other graduate exams.

Forget About "Reading Comprehension"

Your goal on the LSAT is to answer questions and earn points, not to understand a handful of somewhat academic reading passages. The less time you spend reading the passages, the more time you will have for earning points. You need only a superficial understanding of a passage to answer its questions. If you try to gain more than a rough understanding, you'll waste time, become confused, and lose points.

Read for *Ideas*—Ignore the Facts

Did you ever finish a passage on a standardized test only to look up and ask yourself, "What did I just read?" If so, you read the passage too closely. An LSAT passage has a lot of facts but only a few ideas—don't let the details obscure the few important ideas.

If you read too carefully, underlining every other word and wrestling with every detail, you will reach the end of the passage only to discover that you understand nothing. **Read for ideas. Scan later to find facts.**

Don't Get Bogged Down

This point cannot be stressed too highly—you must skim over the details. If you remain unconvinced, here are all the reasons for skimming over the details:

First, passages contain too many facts. You cannot possibly remember all the details crammed into it.

Second, the questions and choices themselves are long and will take quite a bit of time to read.

Third, the questions are mostly *inferential. Inferential* questions ask you to think about the *ideas* rather than the *facts*. Reading closely helps memorization (which you do *not* need), but interferes with understanding (which you *do* need)!

Fourth, the difference between the best and the second-best choices in a question is often hard to distinguish. You will need time to make these hard decisions using our *POE* techniques.

Fifth, and perhaps most important, the more you focus on the details, the more likely you are to fall for traps! We will show you why later.

The House Plan of a Passage

All LSAT passages have the same basic layout. The author has a main idea. Explaining or developing this main idea is her or his main purpose. The author does this by marshalling supporting details, facts, examples, metaphors, and secondary ideas. The author also has an attitude toward the subject of the passage. This attitude is conveyed through tone and style.

Think of the passage as a house about which you're going to be tested. Before the test begins, you're going to be given a few minutes to familiarize yourself with the house and its contents. How will you spend these minutes? Will you spend them memorizing the spices in the spice box in the kitchen, or the books on the shelf in the library? Of course not. You're going to try to develop a general idea of the layout of the house and the arrangement of its contents. Later, if you're asked a question about spices, you'll know where to look for the answer.

You should read a passage in the same way. Concentrate on the general layout of the passage and forget about the details. Later, when you need to find a particular detail in order to answer a question, you'll know where to look for it.

How *Not* to Read

Before we go any further, we need to dismiss several persistent myths about reading on the LSAT.

Myth 1: *You should read the passage slowly so that you will understand everything.*

Wrong! The details will overwhelm you. You are not trying to memorize facts, and you couldn't anyway. You will only waste time that should be spent on the questions. Perhaps worst of all, reading closely increases your chances of being seduced by trap choices. We will *prove* this shortly.

Myth 2: *You should underline key words and important phrases.*

Wrong! This wastes time, and you will not know which phrases are important until after you have finished the passage. The only words worth underlining are the *trigger words,* which we will introduce later.

Myth 3: *You should read between the lines.*

Wrong! You must not read between the lines! Doing so wastes time. True, you will have to apply the ideas of the passage and infer conclusions. The sort of mental leaps you will have to make, however, are rarely major. Don't look for secret meanings.

Myth 4: *You should read the questions before reading the passage.*

Wrong! Students who hear this piece of misguided advice say, "Wow, I never thought of that." With good reason. At best, reading the questions first will give you only a general idea of what the passage is about. This "technique" wastes time, and will confuse you. The only time you should read the questions first is when you hit the last passage with only minutes remaining. We will tell you how to handle this predicament later.

If you are one of those rare test takers who ace passages on standardized tests by reading slowly, underlining every word, and reading between the lines, we can't argue with success. Frankly, though, we know very few students who are successful on the LSAT using such time-consuming and dangerous habits, while we know very many students who have scored high by following our approach.

You will better appreciate the dangers of your normal style of reading if you try it out on the following illustrative passage.

Illustrative Passage: Twelve Minutes Only!

Take 12 minutes (*exactly,* if this quiz is to mean anything) to read this sample passage and answer the questions that follow it. The passage is fairly difficult but you shouldn't find the questions too bad. This sample is about as abstract a passage as you're likely to encounter. We'll refer to this passage and its questions again and again throughout the rest of the chapter as we discuss our techniques.

Don't worry about techniques at this point; we haven't taught you any yet. But time yourself strictly and mark your answers. Check your watch, and begin.

> Any discussion of theories of the firm must
> start with the neoclassical approach, the staple
> diet of modern economists. Developed over the
> last one hundred years or so, this approach can
> (5) be found in any modern-day textbook on
> microeconomics; in fact, in most textbooks it is
> the *only* theory of the firm presented.
>   Neoclassical theory views the firm as a set of
> feasible production plans. A manager presides
> (10) over this production set, buying and selling

CRACKING THE SYSTEM: THE LSAT

inputs and outputs in a spot market and
choosing the plan that maximizes owners'
welfare. Welfare is usually represented by
profit, or by the firm's market value.

(15)   To many economists, this is a caricature of the
modern firm; it is rigorous but rudimentary. At
least three reasons help explain its prolonged
survival. First, the theory lends itself to an
elegant and general mathematical formalization.

(20) Second, it is useful for analyzing how a firm's
production choices respond to exogenous change
in the environment, such as an increase in
wages or a sales tax. Finally, the theory is also
useful for analyzing the consequences of

(25) strategic interaction between firms under
conditions of imperfect competition; for example,
it can help us understand the relationship
between the degree of concentration in an
industry and that industry's output and price

(30) level.

Granted these strengths, neoclassical theory
has some clear weaknesses. It does not explain
how production is organized within a firm, how
conflicts of interest between the firm's various

(35) constituencies—its owners, managers, workers
and consumers—are resolved, or, more generally,
how the manager achieves the goal of profit-
maximization. More subtly, neoclassical theory
begs the question of what defines a given firm

(40) or what determines its boundaries. Since the
theory does not address the issue of each firm's
size or extent, it cannot explain, for example, the
consequences of two firms choosing to merge.
Neoclassical theory describes in rudimentary

(45) terms how firms function, but contributes little to
any meaningful picture of their structure.

Principal-agent theory, an important recent
development, addresses some of the
weaknesses of the neoclassical approach.

(50) Principal-agent theory now recognizes conflicts
of interest between different economic actors.
The theory still views the firm as a production
set, but now a professional manager makes
production choices—such as investment or effort

(55) allocations—that the firm's owners do not

observe. Also, because the manager deals with
the day-to-day operations of the firm, she is
presumed to have information about the firm's
profitability that the owners lack. In addition,
(60) the manager has other goals in mind beyond the
owners' welfare, such as on-the-job perks, an
easy life, empire building, and so on.
    Under these conditions, principal-agent theory
argues that it will be impossible for the owners
(65) to implement their own profit-maximizing plans
directly, through a contract with the manager; in
general, the owners will not even be able to tell
ex post whether the manager has chosen the
right plan. Instead, the owners will try to align
(70) the manager's objectives with their own by
putting the manager on an incentive scheme
such as profit-sharing. Even under an optimal
incentive scheme, however, the manager will put
some weight on her own objectives at the
(75) expense of those of the owners, and conflicting
interests remain. Hence, we have the
beginnings of a managerial theory of the firm.

1. According to the passage, the principal-agent theory of
    the firm suggests that the neoclassical view, despite its
    weaknesses, would be most useful in analyzing which
    one of the following types of firm?

    (A) a one-person entrepreneurial venture
    (B) a non-profit foundation
    (C) a multinational corporation
    (D) a tightly-held partnership
    (E) an absentee-owned service franchise

2. According to the information presented in the passage,
    the neoclassical and principal-agent theories of the firm
    hold which of the following premises in common?

    I. A firm can be viewed as a set of production choices.
    II. Owners of a firm primarily seek to maximize its
        profits.
    III. A firm's production decisions are determined by a
        manager.

    (A) I only
    (B) II only

 (C) I and II only
 (D) I and III only
 (E) I, II, and III

3. According to the passage, the major contribution of the principal-agent theory of the firm is the insight that

 (A) a firm's manager is not concerned with profit-maximization
 (B) the owners of a firm view their welfare in terms of profits
 (C) the manager of a firm is not motivated solely by monetary reward
 (D) the manager of a firm makes production choices
 (E) the neoclassical theory begs the question of what defines a firm

4. It can be inferred from the information in the passage that all of the following would be examples of production decisions the manager of a firm might make EXCEPT

 (A) offering sales discounts
 (B) initiating an overtime shift
 (C) investing in new equipment
 (D) selling a division of the firm
 (E) introducing a new product

5. In this passage the author is primarily concerned with

 (A) outlining the evolution of the principal-agent theory of the firm
 (B) laying the groundwork for a comprehensive theory of the firm
 (C) demonstrating the need for a valid theory of the firm
 (D) showing how an elegant and mathematically formalized theory of the firm is not possible
 (E) discussing the weaknesses of the neoclassical theory of the firm

6. Which one of the following phrases could replace the phrase "a caricature" (line 15) without changing the author's meaning in that sentence?

 (A) an hypothesis
 (B) an abstraction
 (C) an oversimplification

(D) a satire
(E) a prediction

7. Which one of the following titles best summarizes the
main idea of the passage?

(A) The Neoclassical Economic Theory: A Caricature of
the Modern Firm
(B) The Development of the Principal-Agent Theory of the
Firm
(C) Managers: Can They Be Trusted?
(D) Toward a Complete Theory of the Firm
(E) Conflicts of Interest within a Firm

Preliminary Discussion of the Sample Questions

Before we show you how a Princeton Review student would have attacked and
analyzed the sample passage, we'll discuss the questions briefly. We will use
this discussion to introduce important analysis terms in italics. Don't labor over
these terms too much now. They will become clear shortly. We just wanted to
get your feet wet.

Okay then. Let's start with the first question.

1. According to the passage, the principal-agent theory of
the firm suggests that the neoclassical view, despite its
weaknesses, would be most useful in analyzing which
one of the following types of firms?

(A) a one-person entrepreneurial venture
(B) a nonprofit foundation
(C) a multinational corporation
(D) a tightly-held partnership
(E) an absentee-owned service franchise

Here's how to crack it: This is an *inferential* question. *Inferential* questions
require between the lines. *Inferential* questions are more difficult than *explicit*
questions, which can be answered from information stated directly in the passage.

Like many *inferential questions,* this one is difficult. Here's a useful technique for attacking this question: **Arrange the choices along a spectrum: if
there are no meaningful distinctions among the middle choices, the answer will be one of the extremes. If you find a meaningful distinction, look
for the choice that doesn't quite fit in with the others.**

Arranging the choices from "smallest" to "largest," we get something along
the following lines:

A one-person entrepreneurial venture
A tightly-held partnership
An absentee-owned service franchise
A non-profit foundation
A multinational corporation

Since there is no meaningful distinction among the three middle choices, we would expect the answer to lie at one of the extremes. The neoclassical theory either does a good job analyzing a tiny firm, or an enormous one. Eliminate choices (B), (D), and (E).

Looking for the choice that doesn't quite fit with the others suggests the answer is choice (A), the only type of firm with one person. Choices (B), (C), (D), and (E) concern firms with more than one person. So (A) has the edge over (C).

We could stop our analysis here if we were under time pressure in a test situation, but since we're not let's see if we can muscle our way to the answer with some hard thinking.

The principal-agent theory focuses on the conflict between the owners' interests and the manager's interests. We can infer that the neoclassical view would be most useful in analyzing a firm that had no such conflict of interest. There would be no conflict between the owner of a firm and its manager if that person were one and the same. The answer is (A).

2. According to the information presented in the passage, the neoclassical and principal-agent theories of the firm hold which of the following premises in common?

   I. A firm can be viewed as a set of production choices.
  II. Owners of a firm primarily seek to maximize its profits.
 III. A firm's production decisions are determined by a manager.

(A) I only
(B) II only
(C) I and II only
(D) I and III only
(E) I, II, and III

Here's how to crack it: An *explicit Triple True/False* question, a type of *format* question. *Triple True/False* questions are more time consuming than regular questions, but permit you to use efficient *POE*.

Option I: This option is correct. It *paraphrases* the *first sentence* of the second paragraph, and the *trigger word sentence* in the fifth paragraph (line 52). **Any time the test writer goes to the trouble of *paraphrasing* text from the passage, we have a compelling reason to believe that choice is the answer.** The answer must include option I, so eliminate choice (B).

Option II: This option is correct (*last sentence* of the second paragraph, *last sentence* of the fifth paragraph). Some students misread this option to refer to managers. The answer must include option II, so eliminate choices (A) and (D).

Darn. We still have to check the third option. **On many *Triple True/False* questions, efficient *POE* enables you to get by with checking only two of the three options.**

Option III: This option is correct. Support is found in the second paragraph, and in the *trigger word sentence* in the fifth paragraph (line 52) which this option paraphrases. Select choice (E).

Some students misread the *trigger word sentence* beginning in line 52. The manager is still presiding over production, as in the neoclassical view, but the principal-agent theory points out that typically the owners do not observe the manager's production decisions.

Question 2 is a medium-to-difficult question.

3. According to the passage, the major contribution of the principal-agent theory of the firm is the insight that

   (A) a firm's manager is not concerned with profit-maximization
   (B) the owners of a firm view their welfare in terms of profits
   (C) the manager of a firm is not motivated solely by monetary reward
   (D) the manager of a firm makes production choices
   (E) the neoclassical theory begs the question of what defines a firm

Here's how to crack it: An *explicit* question.

(A) Your *outside knowledge* about basic business eliminates this easily *disputable* choice. Of course the manager of a firm is concerned with maximizing profits. The principal agent theory simply points out that this is not the manager's *only* concern. See also the *last sentence* of the fifth paragraph.

(B) Our analysis of *another question* helps here. See question 2, option II. Eliminate.

(C) The answer *paraphrases* the *last sentence* of the fifth paragraph. Also, this choice is *indisputable*.

(D) Once again our analysis of *another question* can be applied. See question 2, option III. You may have been seduced by this choice since it includes a *passage quotation* from the *trigger word sentence* starting on line 52. **Never select a choice simply because it seems to quote from the passage.**

(E) You weren't trapped by this *passage quotation,* were you? If you're not sure about this choice, try the following technique. As we will see shortly, the first step in our approach to analyzing a passage is to isolate the theme of each paragraph. **If the only place a particular fact is mentioned is a paragraph other than the paragraph we should find the answer in, that fact is probably not the answer.**

The principal-agent theory is introduced in the fifth paragraph. This strongly suggests that the answer to this question will *not* be a fact mentioned only in the first four paragraphs. The issue of a firm's boundaries appears in the fourth paragraph only. Eliminate this choice.

Question 3 is a medium question.

4. It can be inferred from the information in the passage that all of the following would be examples of production decisions the manager of a firm might make EXCEPT

    (A) offering sales discounts
    (B) initiating an overtime shift
    (C) investing in new equipment
    (D) selling a division of the firm
    (E) introducing a new product

Here's how to crack it: A *format inferential* question—we'd better watch our step. Using *outside knowledge,* as well as the approach mentioned in Question 1, points to choice (D). If a manager had the authority to sell a division of a firm, he would certainly have the authority to offer sales discounts, start an overtime shift, buy new equipment, or introduce a new product.

Question 4 is a medium question that requires dexterity—we have to remember that the answer is *not* true.

5. In this passage the author is primarily concerned with

    (A) outlining the evolution of the principal-agent theory of the firm
    (B) laying the groundwork for a comprehensive theory of the firm
    (C) demonstrating the need for a valid theory of the firm
    (D) showing how an elegant and mathematically formalized theory of the firm is not possible
    (E) discussing the weakness of the neoclassical theory of the firm

Here's how to crack it: *Theme* questions like this one can be answered quickly if you're short of time: **Check the *first* and *last* sentences of the first paragraph, and the *last sentence* of the entire passage.**

(A) The principal-agent view is not complete since it addresses only some of the weaknesses of the neoclassical view. See the *first sentence* of the fifth paragraph. Eliminate.

(B) The answer paraphrases the *first* and *last sentences* of the passage.

(C) This is superficially plausible, but a *literal reading* of the choice reveals it to be silly. Out.

(D) Let's get real here. Eliminate.

(E) The author does this in order to point the way toward a complete theory of the firm. Eliminate.

Question 5 is an easy-to-medium question.

6. Which one of the following phrases could replace the phrase "a caricature" (line 14) without changing the author's meaning in that sentence?

    (A) an hypothesis
    (B) an abstraction
    (C) an oversimplification
    (D) a satire
    (E) a prediction

Here's how to crack it: A *literary technique* question. Notice that the sentence this phrase appears in is the *first sentence* of the second paragraph. Rigorous but rudimentary: the answer is (C). **Note that the answer to this particular type of *literary technique* question is *not* a synonym for the phrase cited.** *Common sense* tells us that the test writers would not bother asking what the author meant by "caricature" if the answer were "satire."

Question 6 is an easy question.

7. Which one of the following titles best summarizes the main idea of the passage?

    (A) The Neoclassical Economic Theory: A Caricature of
         the Modern Firm
    (B) The Development of the Principal-Agent Theory of the
         Firm
    (C) Managers: Can They Be Trusted?
    (D) Toward a Complete Theory of the Firm
    (E) Conflicts of Interest within a firm

Here's how to crack it: Another *theme question,* and one that can exploit our analysis of *another question.* See our discussion of number 5, the other *theme question.* Choice (D) is the answer.

Question 7 is an easy-to-medium question.

Now that we've analyzed the questions, let's look at the Princeton Review approach to taking apart a passage.

Our Step-by-Step Game Plan for LSAT Reading Passages

Here's our step-by-step game plan for reading the passages and answering the questions:

Step 1: Locate the main idea of the passage.
Step 2: Locate the main idea and the function of each paragraph.
Step 3: Circle *trigger words.*

Step 4: Decide the question order quickly, and attack the easiest question first.

Step 5: Refer back to the passage—if necessary—for details.

Step 6: Use *POE* to select the *best* choice.

Step 1: Locate the Main Idea of the Passage

Remember learning in third grade about *topic sentences?* Well, your third-grade teacher was onto something. **The main idea of LSAT passages tends to be in the last sentence (sometimes the first) of the first paragraph. If not, check the last sentence of the entire passage.**

Let's take a look at the opening line of the illustrative passage to see what we are talking about:

> Any discussion of theories of the firm must start with the neoclassical approach, the staple diet of modern economists.

That's fairly straightforward. The passage will discuss theories of the firm. **Usually, however, the author does not get around to addressing his real issue until the last sentence of the first paragraph or the first sentence of the second paragraph.** Let's drop down to the last *sentence* of the first paragraph:

> Developed over the last one hundred years or so, this approach can be found in any modern-day textbook on microeconomics; in fact, in most textbooks it is the *only* theory of the firm presented.

Okay. The author doesn't seem to be adding too much here. Let's move on.

Step 2: Locate the Main Idea and Function of Each Paragraph

After you grasp the central theme, the only other consideration that concerns you is the *structure* of the passage, the house-plan layout. You want to see how each paragraph relates to the central theme. **You will find the main idea of each paragraph in the *first* and *last* sentences.** Some Princeton Review students find it useful to jot down in the margin a few words to summarize each paragraph. They find doing so forces them to get to the heart of each paragraph. If you had focused on the first and last sentences of the remaining paragraphs as Princeton Review students do, here's what you would have seen of the passage:

> Neoclassical theory views the firm as a set of feasible production plans.
>
> (. . .)

Welfare is usually represented by profit, or by the firm's market value.

To many economists, this is a caricature of the modern firm; it is rigorous but rudimentary.
(. . .)
Finally, the theory is also useful for analyzing the consequences of strategic interaction between firms under conditions of imperfect competition; for example, it can help us understand the relationship between the degree of concentration in an industry and that industry's output and price level.

Granted these strengths, neoclassical theory has some clear weaknesses.
(. . .)
Neoclassical theory describes in rudimentary terms how firms function, but contributes little to any meaningful picture of their structure.

Principal-agent theory, an important recent development, addresses some of the weaknesses of the neoclassical approach.
(. . .)
In addition, the manager has other goals in mind beyond the owners' welfare, such as on-the-job perks, an easy life, empire building, and so on.

Under these conditions, principal-agent theory argues that it will be impossible for the owners to implement their own profit-maximizing plans directly, through a contract with the manager; in general, the owners will not even be able to tell ex post whether the manager has chosen the right plan.
(. . .)
Hence, we have the beginnings of a managerial theory of the firm.

We are not saying you must skip the intervening sentences *entirely*, just don't dwell on them. They usually contain supporting details. Skim them, if you don't feel comfortable skipping over them. But on your initial read of a passage your only concern is extracting the main ideas.

In addition to *first/last sentences,* however, there is one type of sentence you should never skip: *trigger word sentences.*

Step 3: Circle Trigger Words

First and last sentences are not the only ones that contain the author's main ideas. *Trigger word sentences* also contain significant points.

A *trigger word sentence* is any sentence that contains a *trigger word.* The most important *trigger words* are

but	although
however	yet
despite	nevertheless

Every so often you meet variations (*in spite of, notwithstanding, except, nonetheless, on the contrary*), but this list pretty much covers them.

A *trigger word* or *phrase* is one that announces a pivotal reversal in the passage's direction. A *trigger word* is like a hairpin turn: If you aren't paying attention, you'll drive off the road. **Whenever you see a *trigger word,* circle it: Its sentence will very likely contain the answer to a question.** *Trigger* words often appear in the first and last sentences of paragraphs. Such sentences, as we saw in Step 2, are especially crucial.

You don't need to concentrate on these sentences while you are reading the passage; just circle the *trigger words* and go on to the questions. Later, when you come to a hard question and are stuck among several choices, the trigger word sentences will help you make up your mind.

Take a moment now to scan the passage for *trigger words.* Don't read too carefully. With practice, *trigger words* should leap off the page.

Okay, you should have found

but	(line 15)
but	(line 45)
but	(line 53)
however	(line 73)

Did you notice that two of these *trigger words* appear in *first/last sentences*?

Once you've circled the *trigger words,* you are ready to move on to the questions. Before we do, however, let's summarize what we've done. Here is what the illustrative passage looks like after a Princeton Review student gets through with it before attacking the questions:

> Any discussion of theories of the firm must
> start with the neoclassical approach, the staple
> diet of modern economists. Developed over the
> last one hundred years or so, this approach can
> (5) be found in any modern-day textbook on
> microeconomics; in fact, in most textbooks it is
> the *only* theory of the firm presented.
> (10)　　Neoclassical theory views the firm as a set of

popular neoclassical view of firm

feasible production plans. A manager presides
over this production set, buying and selling
inputs and outputs in a spot market and
choosing the plan that maximizes owners'
welfare. Welfare is usually represented by
profit, or by the firm's market value.

outline of neoclassical view

(15)   To many economists, this is a caricature of the
modern firm; it is rigorous but rudimentary. At
least three reasons help explain its prolonged
survival. First, the theory lends itself to an
elegant and general mathematical formalization.
(20)   Second, it is useful for analyzing how a firm's
production choices respond to exogenous change
in the environment, such as an increase in
wages or a sales tax. Finally, the theory is also
useful for analyzing the consequences of
(25)   strategic interaction between firms under
conditions of imperfect competition; for example,
it can help us understand the relationship
between the degree of concentration in an
industry and that industry's output and price
(30)   level.

Strengths of neoclassical view

Granted these strengths, neoclassical theory
has some clear weaknesses. It does not explain
how production is organized within a firm, how
conflicts of interest between the firm's various
(35)   constituencies—its owners, managers, workers
and consumers—are resolved, or, more generally,
how the manager achieves the goal of profit-
maximization. More subtly, neoclassical theory
begs the question of what defines a given firm
(40)   or what determines its boundaries. Since the
theory does not address the issue of each firm's
size or extent, it cannot explain, for example, the
consequences of two firms choosing to merge.
Neoclassical theory describes in rudimentary
(45)   terms how firms function, but contributes little to
any meaningful picture of their structure.

weaknesses of neoclassical view

Principal-agent theory, an important recent
development, addresses some of the
weaknesses of the neoclassical approach.
(50)   Principal-agent theory now recognizes conflicts
of interest between different economic actors.
The theory still views the firm as a production
(55)   set, but now a professional manager makes

a partial improvement: principal-agent view

production choices—such as investment or effort
allocations—that the firm's owners do not
observe. Also, because the manager deals with
the day-to-day operations of the firm, she is
presumed to have information about the firm's
profitability that the owners lack. In addition,
(60) the manager has other goals in mind beyond the
owners' welfare, such as on-the-job perks, an
easy life, empire building, and so on.

Under these conditions, principal-agent theory
argues that it will be impossible for the owners
(65) to implement their own profit-maximizing plans
directly, through a contract with the manager; in
general, the owners will not even be able to tell
ex post whether the manager has chosen the
right plan. Instead, the owners will try to align

principal-agent view: owner/manager conflicts

(70) the manager's objectives with their own by
putting the manager on an incentive scheme
such as profit-sharing. Even under an optimal
incentive scheme, (however) the manager will put
some weight on her own objectives at the
(75) expense of those of the owners, and conflicting
interests remain. Hence, we have the
beginnings of a managerial theory of the firm.

Start of managerial view

Step 4: Decide Question Order Quickly, and Attack the Easiest Question First

The questions following a reading passage are in no particular order, so you want to decide quickly which are easy and which are difficult. Do the easy ones first. That means that you will probably not answer the questions in the order in which they are printed.

Here are our guidelines for deciding which questions are easy:

- *general* questions are easier than *specific* questions
- *explicit* questions are easier than *inferential* questions
- *short-answer choice* questions are easier than *long-answer choice* questions
- *Triple True/False* questions consume more time than do regular questions, but are not necessarily harder
- *EXCEPT/NOT/LEAST* questions are the trickiest and most time-consuming questions

We'll talk about each of these question types later.

A Princeton Review student would have tackled the questions in our illustrative passage more or less in the following order: 6, 5, 7, 3, 2, 1, 4.

Don't waste time trying to decide question order. After all, the point in progressing from the easy to the difficult questions is to save time. As with all Princeton Review techniques, this one takes a little getting used to but pays off on the actual test.

Step 5: Refer Back to the Passage—if Necessary—for Details

You can usually answer the idea questions (*theme* and *inferential*) without refer- ring back to the passage. If you must, refer to the key sentences (*first, last, trigger word*).

To answer detail questions, you may have to refer back to the passage to confirm a fact. Since you know the structure of the passage, the relevant para- graph and line should be easy to find.

How *Not* to Look for Answers

To see how you should not look for answers, put yourself in the place of the test writer. You have selected a passage from a dusty law review article, one with a handful of ideas buried beneath a mountain of details, and written your first question. Now you must write an answer for it. Since you don't want to make things too easy for test takers, you don't want to pluck your answer, word for word, from the text. Instead, you paraphrase the passage, keeping the meaning but changing the words.

Now that you have the correct choice, you need four *incorrect* ones. Writing them won't be as easy as you may think. They have to be wrong, but they also have to be plausible.

How will you make your incorrect choices fulfill these criteria?

By doing the opposite of what you did to disguise your correct choice. The most effective way to make a wrong choice look right is to echo the wording of the passage. How do most test takers look for answers? Easy. The look for choices that echo the wording of the passage. **Most students look for answers in exactly the same way the test writers look for wrong choices!**

In the next step we'll discuss this point in more detail.

Step 6: Use *POE* to Select the *Best* Choice

You've found the idea or the relevant fact with which to answer the question. Now you must avoid the traps and somehow select the *best* answer. If more than one choice seems supportable and you have *any* doubt about which choice is best, then you must find concrete reasons to eliminate all four incorrect choices.

Fortunately, we have an arsenal of techniques with which to identify best answers and eliminate incorrect choices. Best answers have a number of con- sistent characteristics. Let's look at them now. Ideally, the best choice will

- *paraphrase* the wording of the passage
- *not* directly repeat too many words from the passage

- agree with what you know about the subject
- not be simplistic
- agree with the other questions and answers in the passage
- be indisputable

POE Technique #1: Seek Paraphrased Choices

Because the test writers want to make you do more than skim for the answer, they try to phrase the answer with words different from those in the passage. **The answer often *paraphrases* the wording of the passage.** If you cannot decide between two choices, one of which is a paraphrase, go with the paraphrase. **This is true especially on *inferential* questions.**

Just *how much* does the answer *paraphrase* the passage? Not all that much. If the passage says Nietzsche was more a poet than a philosopher, the paraphrased answer will say that Nietzsche was less a philosopher than a poet. If the passage discusses voting patterns among blacks before the 1920s, the *paraphrased* answer might discuss black voting patterns *after* the 1920s.

The following excerpts from the passage illustrate paraphrasing:

<u>Actual Text</u> becomes the	<u>Paraphrased Answer</u>
1. set of production feasible production plans (line 8); production set (line 52)	set of production choices (choice 2I)
2. manager presides over this production set (line 9); manager makes production choices (line 53)	production choices are determined by a manager (choice 2III)
3. manager has other goals (line 60)	manager . . . is not motivated solely (choice 3C)
4. rigorous but rudimentary (line 16)	on oversimplification (choice 6C)

Not all correct answers paraphrase the passage. If the test writer has gone to the trouble of *paraphrasing,* however, that choice is often correct. When in doubt, go with a *paraphrased* choice.

POE Technique #2: Distrust Passage Quotations

You now know that the best choice often *paraphrases* the passage. The flip side is that trap choices often contain *quotations* lifted directly from the passage. The *quotation* in the choice will not be indicated with quotation marks, so you will have to be on guard.

One or two words from the passage repeated in a choice are probably not enough to justify eliminating it. But if a conspicuous phrase from the passage is repeated, you should be cautious about that choice.

How long must the passage quotation in a choice be for you to distrust it? Well, it depends. The key point is this: **If a phrase directly from the passage is long enough to stand out and catch an unwary student's attention, it's very possibly a trap. This is especially true on inferential questions.**

How nice for you that *most* of the reading questions are *inferential*! Since these questions require you to go beyond the passage by drawing a conclusion, you can confidently eliminate wholesale repetitions. If your choice simply repeats the wording of the passage, it cannot have been *inferred*. We'll have more to say about inferential questions later.

Here are examples from our illustrative passage. Compare these with the previous examples of paraphrased choices.

Actual Text	becomes the	Direct Quotation Trap
1. neoclassical theory begs the question of what defines a given firm (line 38)		neoclassical theory begs the question of what defines a given firm (choice 3E)
2. manager makes production choices (line 53)		manager makes production choices (choice 3D)
3. a caricature of the modern firm (line 15)		a caricature of the modern firm (choice 7A)

Watch out the next time you find yourself justifying a choice by saying: "But this choice has to be right! Look, it says the same thing right here!"

This technique is not infallible. Occasionally a choice with a passage quotation *is* the answer.

For example, option II in question 5 of our illustrative passage used a phrase right out of the passage (*unresponsive to abstract demands*) but was nonetheless correct. As with all Princeton Review techniques, this one must be practiced on actual LSATs.

POE Technique #3: Use Outside Knowledge

The LSAT Bulletin contains the following piece of very bad advice:

Answer the questions on the basis of the information provided in the passage and do not rely on outside knowledge.

On the contrary, *outside knowledge* can be extremely useful on the LSAT. The more you know about the way the world works and the way people behave, the better. You can confidently use outside knowledge to eliminate choices you know to be false or absurd. **The simple fact that a statement is true does not necessarily make it a good choice, but a clearly false statement is always a bad choice.** And since the new LSAT now draws its passages from law review articles on social, legal, ethical, historical, and economic issues, outside knowledge is especially helpful.

In the unlikely event that *outside knowledge* may lead you astray, the test writers kindly warn you with a parenthetical disclaimer like the following: "This passage was written in 1980." Such a disclaimer hints that things may have changed since 1980.

Review our analysis of illustrative questions 3 and 4.

POE Technique #4: Use Common Sense

Ask yourself why the question is being asked. The answer to a question may be simple; indeed, as we will see, it often is. It will not, however, be *simplistic*!

To take a very basic example, if a question asks why taxes were raised, the answer will not be, "To raise more money." Review our analysis of question 6 from the illustrative passage.

Many students initially have a hard time with using *outside knowledge* and *common sense* because they focus too much on the passage. Get the big picture. Think!

POE Technique #5: Use Other Questions

If you have narrowed your choices on a question, but reached an impasse, *immediately* move on to another question! More thinking about an ambiguous choice will only increase your confusion, and you have no time to waste. Moreover, other questions often provide clues to the question that baffles you. Review our analysis of questions 3 and 7 from the illustrative passage.

POE Technique #6: Attack Disputable Choices

The answer to every question in the LSAT Reading Passages section almost always fulfills one requirement: **It is *indisputable*! In other words, the answer must be general enough, perhaps even vague enough, so that if every word is taken *literally,* no one will be able to dispute it.**

The LSAS does not want to spend all its time answering angry letters from test takers who quibble with the official answer. The LSAS isn't always successful at avoiding these disputes, but it always tries to do so. A choice that is only "sort of correct" or that you can "see how it could be the answer" isn't good enough.

What makes a choice disputable? **Generally speaking, the more detailed and specific a choice is, the easier it is to dispute, and hence the more likely it is to be wrong.**

Test takers often say, "But I got it down to two choices and they both seemed right!" These students failed to take each and every word literally. Do not read between the lines. If you find yourself saying, "Well, you know, if you look at this choice in a certain way you can see how it might be right," that choice is wrong!

This doesn't mean that a detailed and specific choice is always incorrect. It only means that such choices are the easiest to attack. **If you can't decide between the two plausible choices, start with the choice that gives you specific words that you can attack. Ask yourself why the test writer used each word. Attack that choice by taking every word literally, with *no* interpretation. If that choice survives such ruthless scrutiny, it is probably the answer. If not, the other choice wins by default.**

Some test takers distrust an indisputable choice because it seems *so* indisputable, so obvious, that it couldn't possibly be the right answer to a question on a hard test like the LSAT.

Wrong. Very often the details in a specific answer are there only to make that choice incorrect. **The simpler the choice, the more likely it is to be true. When in doubt, select the choice that can't be disputed.**

Putting the Strategy to Work: Advanced Principles

So far we have described our general strategy for approaching LSAT reading passages. Now we are going to teach you some advanced principles linked to specific types of passages and specific questions.

Handling Opinion Passages

Most LSAT passages deal with opinion. That is, the author is usually making a case for some position rather than merely describing something or rattling off a list of facts.

Keep in mind that the author is never completely for or against anything. Opinion passages are not black and white. If the author disagrees with a position, he will still concede some merit to an opposing viewpoint. In many LSAT reading passages, the author's intention is to distinguish his position from conventional wisdom—an opposing position held by almost everyone else. The author spells out the conventional wisdom in order to knock it down. **Always be careful to separate the author's opinion from his portrayal of the conventional wisdom.**

Opinion Passages—How to Spot Conventional Wisdom

You know that you must read carefully to distinguish the author's opinion from conventional wisdom—what other people think on a subject. The following lines illustrate how an author might introduce conventional wisdom:

Many efforts in the past to promote international
cooperation have been advocated because . . .

The consensus about the negative impact of taxes on
residential investment . . .

Most people will not support a political candidate
unless he or she . . .

In the past, the scientific community has argued . . .

In all these quotations the author is spelling out a position with which he disagrees. You will never find an LSAT passage in which the author says, "In the past, most people believed in the traditional theory. They were right then, and they're right today." When a paragraph begins in a similar vein, you know that very likely the author is about to disagree with this conventional wisdom.

Theme Questions

Theme questions include the passage's main idea, its purpose, and its tone. A common variant is the infamous *best title* question. We will consider each of these separately.

Handling Main Idea Questions

Main idea questions are easy to spot. Here are a few examples:

- Which of the following statements best summarizes the
  central idea of the passage?
- Which one of the following is the primary question this
  passage attempts to answer?
- The author's main idea in this passage is that . . .

These questions are rarely difficult if you use *POE*. The main idea will appear, as you know, in a *first/last/trigger word sentence*. Eliminate the absurd choices. The main idea will be general without straying from the subject matter. Main idea questions usually *paraphrase* the passage.

When you narrow your selection to a few choices, compare them to each other in an elimination round. Say you have it down to choices (A), (B), and (C). First compare choices (A) and (B). If you *had* to choose only one, which would it be? Then match the winner against the choice (C) and repeat the procedure.

Handling Best Title Questions

Many students don't quite know how to approach "best title" questions. Such questions appear to be so much a "matter of opinion."

They aren't. The correct "title" will capture the general theme of the passage, without being too specific. Focus on the *first/last sentences* of the first two paragraphs, and especially the *last sentence* of the entire passage.

Handling Primary Purpose Questions

Related to main idea questions, primary purpose questions are also easy to spot:

- The author's primary purpose is to . . .
- In the passage, the author is primarily concerned with . . .

The author's primary purpose is simple: to convey the main idea. **Focus on the verb** (*to argue, to convince, to describe*). Primary purpose questions are even easier than main idea questions.

Handling Author's Attitude/Tone Questions

Author's attitude/tone questions come in two basic variations:

- The author's attitude regarding . . . is best characterized as . . .
- The author's tone in the discussion of . . . is best described as . . .

Attitude/tone questions have very short answer choices, so these are the easiest questions to answer.

Begin by deciding whether the author's attitude/tone is positive, negative, or neutral. Eliminate a few choices, then match the remaining choices against each other, elimination style. Beware extreme choices.

One warning: Make sure you deal with the author's attitude toward the specific topic being asked about. For instance, the author's attitude toward big business could be negative, but his attitude toward entrepreneurs could be positive.

Handling Inferential Questions

Inferential questions are worded in a number of ways:

- It can be inferred that . . .
- The passage suggests . . .
- The author implies that . . .

- That passage probably . . .
- The author would probably agree that . . .

Inferential questions ask you to go beyond the text. To answer them you will have to draw probable conclusions, make predictions, or fill in gaps in the author's analysis. *Inferential* questions often have *paraphrased* answers, so they tend to involve more thought—and time. Do them after you have done the theme questions and the explicit questions.

Handling Explicit/Detail Questions

These questions often begin, "According to the passage . . ." Some details lie in the key sentences (*first/last/trigger*), but you may need to refer back to the passage to hunt for the details you skimmed over in your initial read. **Beware: some apparently explicit questions are veiled inferential questions.** Examine illustration question number 1.

A special type of detail question asks you to refer to a specific line.

Handling Line Number Questions

Just a warning about these: if a question refers to line 10, the answer might be anywhere from line 5 to 15. Always consider the *context* of the quotation.

Format Questions

There are two types of format questions: *EXCEPT* questions, and *Triple True/False* questions. Both are time-consuming.

Handling *LEAST/EXCEPT/NOT* Questions

You will sometimes be asked questions that require you to determine which of the five choices is *LEAST* likely to be true, or you may be offered five choices and told that all are true *EXCEPT* one. Such questions are generally easy to spot, because the crucial word is usually printed in capital letters. **Beware: the crucial word is sometimes left in lowercase.**

These questions can be very confusing, because they ask you to find a choice that is, in effect, incorrect. **If a passage has a question like this, answer it last. If time is running short, skip the question entirely.**

Handling *Triple True/False* Questions

You will frequently find questions on the LSAT with three Roman numerals. We call these *Triple True/False* questions because you are really being asked to determine whether each of the three statements is true or false. You will receive credit only if you're right about every one of the statements. Because of this, these questions are very time-consuming. If a passage has a question like this, we suggest you do it last.

Most students mechanically check the first option, then the second option, and then the third option. Don't.

Before you begin, scan the options for the one that seems easiest to prove or disprove. Start with that one. Decide whether the option is true or false. Then use *POE* to eliminate as many choices as possible. Decide which of the two remaining options is easier to prove or disprove, and repeat the process.

The important point about these questions is that quite often you need not check all the options. By the way, a *Triple True/False EXCEPT* question is easier than a regular *EXCEPT* question since you have only three options to consider instead of four or five.

Handling Literary Technique Questions

These questions are almost like mini-primary purpose questions. They concern the literary and argumentation techniques the author uses to present his case:

- It can be inferred that the author of the passage most likely uses the word "value" (line 33) because . . .
- The author contrasts the examples of the capitalist and socialist societies in order to . . .
- In criticizing the opponents of decentralization, the author does all of the following EXCEPT . . .
- The author refers to the Fifth Amendment in order to . . .

Why does the author do anything? Either to support his own case or to criticize the conventional wisdom. Use *common sense*. These questions are rather easy.

A Note on Handling Argument Questions

There is an entire section of the LSAT devoted to Arguments. Simple argument questions sometimes appear on reading passages, too:

- Which of the following, if true, would support the author's conclusion that . . .
- Which of the following, if true, would weaken the author's argument that . . .

We will show you how to tackle these questions in the next chapter on the Arguments section.

How to Approach this Section

First, get a one-minute overview of the entire section by glancing at the first few lines of each passage. This should give you an idea of the difficulty of the passages.

Since any order of difficulty is rough only, *you* must decide the order in which to complete the passages. Save the most difficult passage for last, it will probably be one of the last passages in the section.

How do you decide which passage is the most difficult? The three factors to weigh are

- How difficult does the subject matter seem?
- How difficult do the questions seem?
- Does the section seem to be arranged in order of difficulty?

Weigh these factors together—easy subject matter may precede difficult questions, or easy questions may follow difficult subject matter.

Common Mistakes

The most common mistake test takers make is finishing the section. If you make more than two errors on any given passage, or more than six errors on the entire section, you're moving too quickly.

Another mistake is spending too much time on the passage and too little time on the questions. Having wasted time on the passage, and emerging from it confused, test takers have precious little time for *POE* techniques.

Pacing

Four passages in 35 minutes means you have about 9 minutes per passage. For most test takers this is not enough. Most test takers need 10 to 12 minutes to work through the passage and its questions conscientiously.

Given that you will *not* have time to use *POE* on *each* question, you will probably have to omit one passage. (Don't forget to guess answers to the questions, though.) In fact, omitting a passage is an excellent strategy for most students. Having nine extra minutes to spend on the other passages can make a big difference.

If you do omit a passage, be sure to omit an entire passage rather than to omit one or two questions on each of several passages. Reading the passages is the most time-consuming part of these problems. Once you've invested your time in reading a passage, you should get your money's worth by answering all the questions.

The one exception to this advice may be when you have a couple of minutes remaining. Let's say you are almost finished with the third passage. You have saved the difficult inferential questions and a *Triple True/False* question for last. You might be better off punting these last few questions and moving on to the final passage for a few easy main-idea questions. Even the most difficult passage should have one or two of these.

If you turn to the last passage with two minutes to go, proceed directly to the main idea and primary purpose questions. You should not waste time reading the entire passage, since you will not then have any time for the questions.

In summary, most test takers should budget their 35 minutes roughly as follows:

↓

Time 1:00   section overview (read the first couple of lines of each passage; decide which passage to do last and which to skip entirely)

↓

Time 11:00   first passage (3 minutes on the passage; 7 minutes on the questions)

↓

Time 22:00   second passage (3 minutes on the passage; 8 minutes on the questions)

↓

Time 33:00   third passage (3 minutes on the passage; 8 minutes on the questions—possibly skip the last couple of long/hard questions here to do the easier general questions from the fourth passage)

↓

Time 45:00   fourth passage (30 seconds on the first/last sentences of the first couple of paragraphs and the last sentence of the entire passage; 30 seconds on an easy theme question or two; final seconds filling in all remaining blanks)

(Note: Depending on your goal and your reading skill, you may have to budget more or less time for each passage. As we discussed in the Basic Principles chapter, **your initial overview should include these pacing considerations, before time trouble clouds your judgment.**)

Guessing Strategy

On the questions you don't get to, remember to fill in the blanks. If the correct answer choices were randomly distributed, it wouldn't matter how you guessed. Surprisingly, however, the test writers have allowed a bias to creep into the answers, a bias that you can exploit.

On reading questions:

- Longer choices have an edge over shorter choices—**when, and only when, all POE attempts fail, favor the longest choice.** (Don't bother counting words, just eyeball the choices.)
- On *Triple True/False* questions, all three options are usually NOT correct —**when, and only when, all POE attempts fail, avoid I, II, and III.**
- The central letters (choices B, C, and D) have a slight edge over the extreme letters (choices A and E)—**when, and only when, all POE attempts fail, guess "toward" choices (C) and (D).**
- Three letters "in a row" are not that rare, but you'll almost never find four

—when, and only when, all *POE* attempts fail, avoid a letter if it would create four in a row. If you're absolutely sure that questions 17, 18, and 19 are (D), (D), and (D), the odds are *overwhelmingly* against question 20 being a (D).

Although these biases are significant, they should *not* override *POE* considerations. For example, if the choice is between (A), which is indisputable, and (C), which is disputable, go with (A).

These rules should be used *only* when all else fails—that is, when your 35 minutes is just about up and you're scrambling to fill in any remaining questions you *absolutely* couldn't decide using *POE* or didn't get to. There is also the chance the test writers will catch on to these biases and eliminate them.

Sometimes you find yourself with only seconds to go and, say, half a dozen unanswered questions. If so, use the following rule: **Scan your answer sheet for that section's column and in the remaining blanks, fill in *the* letter that has appeared the least on the questions you've already answered, giving slight priority to choices (C) and (D).**

This last-resort guessing rule is fail-safe. It will work even if the test writers catch on to the biases we just mentioned and randomize the answer choices and characteristics.

Summary

1. The reading section on your LSAT will contain four passages and 26 to 28 questions.

2. LSAT passages are drawn from law review articles but do not require legal knowledge on your part.

3. LSAT passages are on social, legal, economic, ethical, and historical topics.

4. If you read the passages slowly and carefully, your score will suffer.

5. Your goal is to answer questions, not to understand the passages.

6. Most students could benefit from omitting one of the four passages entirely.

7. Every reading passage and the questions that follow it contain clues that will enable you to eliminate incorrect choices and find the answers. Your job is to find these clues.

8. There are four persistent myths about reading on the LSAT:
Myth 1: You should read the passage slowly.
Myth 2: You should underline key words and phrases.
Myth 3: You should read between the lines.
Myth 4: You should read the questions before reading the passage.

9. We have a step-by-step strategy for reading passages on the LSAT:
Step 1: Locate the main idea of the passage.
Step 2: Locate the main idea and the function of each paragraph.

Step 3: Circle *trigger words*.

Step 4: Decide the question order quickly and attack the easiest question first.

Step 5: Refer back to the passage—if necessary—for details.

Step 6: Use *POE* to select the *best* choice.

10. There are four basic types of questions on the LSAT. Do them in the following order.

   1. *Theme* questions
   2. *Explicit* questions
   3. *Inferential* questions
   4. *Format* questions

11. Use *POE* aggressively: Cross out incorrect choices and "back into" the answer.

12. Use common sense to eliminate obviously incorrect choices.

13. Attack disputable statements. Correct choices are indisputable.

14. Seek paraphrased answers. Long direct quotations from the passage may be traps.

15. Use outside knowledge: correct LSAT answers are not false, nor do they conflict with your general understanding of the world and people's behavior.

16. Use other questions and answers within a passage to supply clues for questions that baffle you.

17. The main ideas tend to occur in *first* and *last* sentences of paragraphs. Treat long sentences like paragraphs and look at the first and last parts.

18. Remember *trigger words*. *Trigger word* sentences usually contain answers.

19. Don't mistake the author's opinion for the conventional wisdom he mentions only to refute.

20. Be aggressive on main idea/purpose and author's attitude/tone questions.

21. The answer to a line-number question may not be found in the specific line(s) cited.

22. Postpone answering the tricky *LEAST/EXCEPT/NOT* questions.

23. *Triple True/False* questions are time-consuming but good for methodical *POE*.

24. Before you dive into the first passage, get an overview of the section. Decide which passage is the most difficult and do it last. You may want to omit it entirely, going for a few of the theme questions in the remaining seconds.

25. If you're almost out of time, fill in all remaining blanks by guessing (B), (C), or (D), whichever has appeared least on the questions you've completed.

CHAPTER 4

Arguments

Each of the two Arguments sections consists of some 20 minipassages, or arguments. Each argument has one or two questions, so each section totals about 25 questions.

Before we begin, take a moment to read the instructions to this section:

Directions: The questions in this section require you to evaluate the reasoning contained in brief statements or passages. In some questions, each of the choices is a conceivable solution to the particular problem posed. However, you are to select the one that is best; that is, the one that does not require you to make what are by commonsense standards implausible, superfluous, or incompatible assumptions. After you have chosen the answer, blacken the corresponding space on the answer sheet.

These are the directions that will appear on your LSAT. Review them now. They will not change in substance. Don't waste time and points by reading them in the test room. You shouldn't even glance at them when you take the test.

What You Will See

Arguments range in length from 20 to 100 words. Arguments represent a diverse range of works, including philosophical, literary, and critical pieces; political speeches; informal dialogues; articles on science, the humanities, and the social sciences; even advertisements.

We refer to the minipassages in these sections as arguments, but technically speaking, some of the passages are actually *explanations*. Others consist of nothing more than a list of statements. Our approach to arguments differs in some key respects from our approach to reading passages. We will point out the differences and similarities as we go along, and summarize them at the end of this chapter.

What Arguments Test

These sections test your ability to understand, to analyze, and to criticize an argument. The LSAT Bulletin lists ten aspects of logical and critical reasoning:

1. identifying the main point of an argument
2. identifying the premises and assumptions of an argument
3. drawing conclusions from given evidence or premises
4. inferring the logical direction of an argument
5. applying the principles of one argument to another argument
6. recognizing methods of argument and persuasion
7. evaluating an argument
8. distinguishing facts from opinions
9. analyzing the evidence of a position
10. weighing claims critically

In short, arguments test your ability to reason.

What Arguments Do *Not* Test

These sections do *not* require any formal knowledge of logic or logical terminology. Don't be intimidated by the tone of some of the questions. Like all sections of the LSAT, the Arguments sections pretend to be a little less straightforward than they are. In fact, the sort of logic tested in this section is so basic that we were tempted to characterize the reasoning as common sense. **Because arguments do not require formal logic, any choice that sounds as if a philosophy professor wrote it is probably incorrect.**

Will Any College Courses Prepare Me for Arguments?

While these sections do not require formal logic, you do need to be familiar with certain basic logic terms. If you took a course in logic or statistics (which helps with some types of arguments), great—you have a head start. If not, this chapter covers everything you need to handle any LSAT argument. If your only motivation is scoring well on the LSAT, take other electives.

How You Will Improve Your Arguments Score

Your thinking habits have developed over many years. Thinking has become so natural that you may be only dimly aware of the actual processes involved. You think all the time. Unfortunately, sloppy thinking is more common than sloppy grammar. Even when people reason correctly, many are unable to say just *how* they arrived at the answer.

The Princeton Review comes to the rescue. In this chapter we will teach you all the logic you need to know. Our techniques will enable you to

1. understand the basic structure of an LSAT argument
2. employ a rigorous plan of attack
3. find correct answers even when you can't follow the argument

Our discussion in this chapter borrows (and sometimes distorts) a few terms and concepts from the study of formal logic. Many of our comments are specific to arguments *as they appear on the LSAT*. We will review only that part of logic and argumentation necessary to do well on the LSAT, and we will cover that information from the LSAT point of view.

We say this so as not to antagonize any fastidious philosophy majors out there. With the questions and choices to help you, you have little actual knowledge to master.

How to Read This Chapter

Since you know how to argue, you may be tempted to take this chapter for granted. Don't! Work through this chapter as you do the others—thoroughly. Especially now that your performance on Arguments determines half your LSAT score!

What Is an Argument?

The word *argument* may call to mind an image of the sorts of debate that develop in the bleachers at a baseball game or at the local bar around closing time. These, of course, are not what the LSAT tests. For our purposes, an argument can be defined as a conclusion supported by premises and assumptions.

In each passage, the author will try to prove something—his *conclusion*. He will support his conclusion with stated reasons, or *premises*. His argument will also be supported by unstated premises, or *assumptions*. Just how these premises and assumptions support the author's conclusion constitutes the *reasoning*.

Your job will be to analyze each argument—to take it apart and see how it works. You may be asked to identify the conclusion that the author has drawn from his premises; you may be asked to supply an unstated conclusion for him. Other questions ask you to identify a premise the author uses, or to supply an unstated premise (assumption) that the author uses. Finally, some questions may ask you to analyze the reasoning by which the author has used his premises to support his conclusion.

The Parts of an Argument

Let's break down an argument into its three basic parts:

The conclusion: The conclusion is the point or the main idea of the argument. It is what the author is trying to prove. The conclusion may be unstated.

The premises: The premises are the reasons or the evidence the author gives to back up the conclusion. Some premises are unstated; you find them between the lines. Unstated premises are called *assumptions*.

The reasoning: The reasoning is *how* the author uses the premises to support the conclusion. The reasoning is the logical principles the author appeals to when saying that the premises support the conclusion. It is the glue that holds the argument together. The two main types of reasoning are *deductive* and *inductive*. (We'll explain the difference between deductive and inductive reasoning later.)

Let's Get Dumb for a Minute

Take a look at the following very simple example. You won't really find a question like this on the LSAT, but thinking about it will help you get a handle on what the test writers expect you to do on this part of the test.

Suppose that two college seniors are sitting together in the student union. Here's what student A says to student B:

> I'll make a better lawyer than you will because I have more compassion for my fellow man.

This is student A's argument. He's offering a conclusion ("I'll make a better lawyer") on the basis of a premise ("I have more compassion"). His argument also depends on several assumptions. These assumptions aren't stated, but they're there anyway. For one thing, student A assumes that both he and student B will become lawyers. For another thing, he assumes that compassion has something to do with being a lawyer.

Would it be possible to weaken student A's argument by adding a new piece of information? Certainly. Suppose we pointed out that student A did so poorly on the LSAT last month that he has no hope of being admitted to law school, while student B has already been accepted by Yale.

This, in very crude form, is the sort of analysis you will have to do in the Arguments section of the LSAT. LSAT arguments will be harder to analyze, of course, but the basic principles will be roughly the same.

Now, Back to Reality

Before we introduce our strategies for analyzing LSAT arguments and answering the questions about them, we need to lay a little more groundwork. We've already defined an LSAT argument as a conclusion supported by stated premises and unstated assumptions. Now we're going to expand our definition. We're going to tell you more about the structure of LSAT arguments so that you can understand how the different parts work together. The more you understand about the structure of an argument, the better able you'll be to use the techniques we'll teach you later on.

The Structure of LSAT Arguments

If you analyze the sentence structure of LSAT arguments, you'll find two basic structures:

premise, premise, premise, conclusion

or

conclusion, premise, premise, premise

Note that the conclusion usually appears in the first or last sentence of the argument. Occasionally, the conclusion is unstated. The assumptions, of course, are unstated.

LSAT arguments are not formal arguments written by philosophers. Most LSAT arguments are informal. They may contain redundancies, extraneous information, rhetorical questions, or even concessions. Some are incomplete. To complicate matters, their wording is often vague or ambiguous. You may see arguments that look like this:

premise, redundancy, redundancy, *conclusion,* redundancy

or

premise, extraneous information, concession, rhetorical question

Ignore this other stuff. **Your primary aim in every argument question is to reduce the passage to the basic structure of *conclusion* supported by *premises.*** Once you identify this structure, everything else falls into place.

Having discussed the basic terms you need to know, we're ready to present our general approach to handling argument questions.

Our Step-by-Step Approach to Arguments

Here's the outline of our general strategy for handling arguments:

Step 1: Read the question.
Step 2: Read the argument.
Step 3: Find the conclusion, then work backward to the premises.
Step 4: Diagram the argument (if necessary) and note the type of reasoning.
Step 5: Attack the choices using *POE*.

Let's apply our approach to a sample argument, after which we will discuss the steps in detail. As always, work through the argument on your own before reading our analysis.

Putting the Strategy to Work: Sample Argument No. 1

Questions 1–2

A growing number of ecologists have begun to recommend lifting the ban on the hunting of leopards and on the international trade of leopard skins. Why, then, do I continue to support the protection of leopards? For the same reason that I oppose the hunting of people. Admittedly, there are far too many human beings on this planet to qualify us for inclusion on the list of endangered species. Still, I doubt the same ecologists endorsing the resumption of leopard hunting would use that fact to recommend the hunting of human beings.

1. Which of the following is the main point of the argument above?

   (A) The ban on leopard hunting should not be lifted.
   (B) Human beings are a species like any other animal, and we should be placed on the endangered species list in view of the threat of nuclear annihilation.
   (C) Hunting of animals, whether or not an endangered species, should not be permitted.
   (D) Ecologists do not consider human beings a species, much less an endangered species.
   (E) Ecologists cannot be trusted where emotional issues like hunting are involved.

2. Which of the following, if true, would most weaken the author's argument?

(A) Human beings might, in fact, be placed on the list of endangered species.

(B) It is impossible to ensure complete compliance with any international hunting ban.

(C) Leopards, now dangerously overpopulated, cannot be supported by their ecosystems.

(D) Despite the growing number of ecologists supporting a repeal of the ban on leopard hunting, most still support it.

(E) The international ban on leopard hunting was instituted before leopards became an endangered species.

Cracking Sample Arguments No. 1: Step 1

The main point of an argument is the author's conclusion. The first question is a *Find-the-Conclusion* question. The second question is a *Weaken-the-Conclusion* question. To weaken an argument, weaken the conclusion. **The strongest way to weaken a conclusion is to find a reason for believing the opposite.** If the author supports protecting leopards, you're looking for a choice that would *endanger* leopards.

Cracking Sample Argument No. 1: Steps 2 & 3

The author tells us that some ecologists believe that leopards should be hunted. The author puts their view first so that he can disagree with it. The author believes that leopards should *not* be hunted.

Cracking Sample Argument No. 1: Step 4

The author is drawing an analogy between the obvious ban on the hunting of human beings and the ban on leopard hunting.

Cracking Sample Argument No. 1: Step 5

Question 1: Choice (A) is the answer. Choice (C) goes too far. The author is not arguing that all hunting should be prohibited. *Watch out for choices that generalize beyond the scope of the author's claim.* (The other choices are more or less silly.)

Question 2: We're looking for a reason not to accept the author's argument. In other words, we're looking for a choice that favors the repeal of the ban on leopard hunting.

Choices (A), (D), and (E) attempt to weaken the argument by raising minor objections to the premise. Quibbling with an author's premises does not greatly weaken his argument.

Choice (B) is indisputable and hence wrong since it must be true already. Moreover, this choice does not support the hunting of leopards.

Choice (C) is the answer. If leopards are dangerously overpopulated, hunting them would reduce their population.

Now that you've seen our strategy in action, let's examine each of its steps.

Step 1: Read the Question

The question tells you how you must read the argument, and how deeply you should analyze it. For example, if a question asks you to criticize a flawed argument, it helps you to know this! If the argument includes more than one question, read all of them. Not the answer choices, just the question(s).

Step 2: Read the Argument Carefully

Unlike our approach to reading passages, do not skim through the middle of an argument. Read the entire argument carefully.

Step 3: Isolate the Conclusion, Then Work Backward to the Premises

Use one of the methods mentioned earlier. Remember: **Sometimes the conclusion is unstated, and you must provide one.**

This step may not be necessary in all types of questions. Analyze only as much of the argument as you need to answer the question.

Step 4: Diagram the Argument If Necessary, and Note the Type of Reasoning

The main idea can often be reduced to one sentence. Summarize the argument in one sentence and diagram this sentence. Diagraming forces you to understand the argument. You can skip this step in the actual exam if you know what you're doing. We've said this before: **Analyze only as much of the argument as you need to answer the question.**

Knowing what type of reasoning (deductive/inductive) the author is using helps you anticipate what is being tested by the question. We will discuss the various types of reasoning shortly.

Step 5: Attack the Choices Using *POE*

This is especially important since the difference between the best choice and the second-best choice is often agonizingly subtle. If you are stuck, however, move on quickly. Return to the question later if time permits, when you have a better perspective on the choices.

Using *POE* on Arguments

The directions to these sections warn you of the critical importance of the process of elimination (italics supplied):

> Directions: The questions in this section require you to evaluate the reasoning contained in brief statements or passages. *In some questions, each of the choices is a conceivable solution to the particular problem posed.* However, you are to select the one that is <u>best</u>; that is, the one that does not require you to make what are by common-sense standards implausible, superfluous, or incompatible assumptions. After you have chosen the best answer, blacken the corresponding space on the answer sheet.

When stuck between two or more choices, examine each one carefully and ask yourself why it was worded in this particular way. Why did the test writer use one phrase in this choice but another phrase in that choice? **Take each word literally. The answer is simply the choice you couldn't eliminate.**
     Here are some guidelines:

1. Choose the simple choice over the complicated one.
2. Choose the choice that stays within the precise scope of the argument over one that generalizes beyond the argument.
3. Watch out for extreme words like *all, always, never,* and *everyone.* Such words are often included to make a choice correct or incorrect.

The Informal Wording of Arguments

LSAT arguments are primarily informal. In fact, they are often disorganized and poorly written. The language of these informal arguments sometimes complicates your analysis.
     First, simple sentences are sometimes vague. Consider the following statement (which did not appear on a real LSAT):

> *Lawyers are crooks.*

Does that mean that *all* lawyers are crooks? Perhaps it means that *most* lawyers are crooks, or that the average lawyer is a crook, or that even the best lawyer is a crook, or that lawyers as a class are crooks. Just what *does* it mean? When in doubt on the LSAT, take every word literally: All lawyers are crooks.
     Let's consider another statement:

> *All lawyers are not crooks.*

Does this mean that all lawyers are decent, law-abiding citizens? Or does it mean that all lawyers are not crooks, but that some lawyers *are* crooks?

These examples illustrate the pitfalls of colloquial language. Remember our maxim: **When in doubt, take every word *literally*.**

Simplify the Language

Even valid arguments are sometimes phrased awkwardly. If you encounter such an argument, simplify the wording. For example, one argument began as follows:

> *There are few scientists who*
> *would not be surprised . . .*

This could have been expressed more lucidly as

> *Most scientists would be surprised . . .*

Do not *over*simplify the wording! When you simplify the wording of an argument, do not change its meaning.

Use Our Reading Passage Techniques Cautiously

When we discussed reading passages, we gave you a number of *POE* techniques: seek paraphrases, avoid direct quotations, use outside knowledge, use common sense, attack disputable statements.

Arguments look like brief reading passages, but there are important differences. For example, unlike reading passages, many arguments are fallacious. Because of this fact, and because of the more fixed structure of arguments, use our reading techniques cautiously. (See the chapter summary for a more detailed comparison of techniques.)

Logic 101: All the Logic You Need for the LSAT

Although the Arguments section does not require knowledge of formal logic, it does require some familiarity with basic terms and concepts from logic. In the following pages we will cover everything you need to know.

The Parts of an Argument: The Conclusion

The conclusion is the point of the argument. It is what the author is claiming, and trying to prove with the premises. Roughly speaking, the conclusion is the main idea of the argument.

The first step in analyzing any argument is to isolate the conclusion. **Be sure to identify its precise scope.** For example, in an argument about gas mileage, be sure to determine whether the author is talking about the mileage of all forms of transportation or merely that of automobile transportation. Misreading the scope of the conclusion is a common error. We will say more about this when we discuss *POE* on arguments.

As we noted earlier, the conclusion may be unstated. Most LSAT arguments, however, state their conclusions. You can locate the conclusion in many ways.

How to Find the Conclusion

To identify the conclusion, ask yourself, *What is the author trying to make me believe?* That is the conclusion.

Asking this question won't always lead you to the conclusion. When it doesn't, you should try the methods listed below. One of the first two will usually do the trick.

1. **Look at the first and last sentences.** As the word itself suggests, the conclusion is often stated in the last sentence of the argument. If not, check the first sentence. But remember: The conclusion can appear at any point in an informal argument.

2. **Look for Conclusion Signal Words.** The conclusion is often revealed by what logicians call *signal words, cue words,* or *indicator words.* A partial list of conclusion signal words and phrases includes

so	implies
therefore	shows that
accordingly	indicates that it
hence	follows that

   On the LSAT, any proposition *following* these words is the conclusion. Conversely, propositions *preceding* these words are—you guessed it—the premises. Consider the following example:

I want to lose weight	so	I should go on a diet.
(premise)	(signal word)	(conclusion)

   Of course, the conclusion is not always tipped off by conclusion words (I should go on a diet to lose weight).

3. **Answer any rhetorical questions.** The author sometimes poses a rhetorical question like *Should elderly people go without medical care?* The conclusion will be the answer to any such question.

4. **Look for the controversial.** The conclusion must be supported by other statements. It cannot be an isolated statement or a simple assertion. Remember: The conclusion must be something worth arguing about.

5. **Work backward from the premises.** If you know a premise but are unsure about whether a statement is the conclusion, ask yourself if the premise makes the statement more likely to be true. If so, the statement is the conclusion. **The conclusion should be actively supported by the premises, not merely permitted by them.**

6. **Identify the author.** If you can identify the author, ask yourself what this author would be trying to make you believe. Is the author an advertiser, a politician, a scientist? What would such a person be arguing for?

7. **Look for the disputable.** The conclusion of an argument is probably *not* indisputable. If it were, why would the author be arguing to convince you of it?

Putting the Strategy to Work: Sample Argument No. 2

1. Many scientists and researchers equate addiction with physical dependence. This interpretation is fallacious. It fails to account for the most problematic aspect of addiction: drug-seeking behavior. Physical dependence is nothing more than the adaptive result of taking certain chemicals repeatedly. The distinction between dependence and addiction can clearly be seen in the usual failure of detoxification—the supervised gradual withdrawal of the drug—to cure addicted human beings.

    Which of the following can be properly inferred from the statements above?

    (A) Detoxification is usually able to cure human beings of a physical dependence on drugs.
    (B) Addiction is not an adaptive result.
    (C) Addiction, while not completely understood, has nothing to do with physical dependence.
    (D) Drug-seeking behavior is a consequence of physical dependence as well as of addiction.
    (E) It is impossible to completely and permanently cure addicted human beings.

Cracking Sample Argument No. 2: Step 1

Sometimes *Supply-a-Conclusion* questions use the word *infer*.

Cracking Sample Argument No. 2: Steps 2 & 3

The author states his main idea in the last line: *That detoxification does not cure addicted human beings but distinguishes addicted human beings from those who are merely physically dependent.*

Cracking Sample Argument No. 2: Step 4

The author is using deductive reasoning.

Cracking Sample Argument No. 2: Step 5

(A) This is the answer. If the author argues that addiction is not the same thing as physical dependence because detoxification does not cure addicted human beings, we can infer that detoxification *does* cure human beings of physical dependence.

(B) Addiction may be an adaptive result according to the author, or it may not. We don't know, since the author does not cite this as a distinguishing factor. Eliminate.

(C) If drug addiction and physical dependence had little in common, why would the author be trying to show what distinguishes one from the other? Moreover, this choice is too absolute. Eliminate.

(D) The first line contradicts this. Eliminate.

(E) This is possible, but a little too extreme. The author suggests that it is extremely difficult to cure human beings of addiction, but we cannot infer that it is impossible to cure them. Eliminate.

The Parts of an Argument: The Premises

A premise is evidence for the claim. The premises of the argument justify the conclusion. A premise supports the conclusion, so a premise itself is usually unsupported.

The author advances each premise as true. Unless the argument is blatantly flawed (the flaws of most LSAT arguments are subtle), the premises will be plausible.

How to Find the Premises

1. **Work backward from the conclusion.** Once you isolate the conclusion, the other statements are either premises, counter-considerations, or fillers. Ask yourself whether the statement supports the conclusion. If so, the statement is a premise.

2. **Look for premise signal words.** You saw that conclusions are sometimes revealed by conclusion words. Indicator words can also tip off the premises. A partial list of premise words includes:

since	in view of
because	given that
suppose	if
assume	

The premises often *follow* a premise word. For example:

I should go on a diet   because   I want to lose weight.
   (conclusion)   (signal word)   (premise)

Notice that the conclusion here *precedes* the premise word. Of course, you can rewrite the argument so that the conclusion also follows the premise word (Because I want to lose weight, I should go on a diet).

3. **Look for isolated statements.** Remember: The conclusion is supported by premises, but the premises are generally unsupported and thus isolated statements. That is one way to distinguish a premise from the conclusion.

The Parts of an Argument: The Unstated Premises, or Assumptions

As we noted earlier, assumptions are unstated premises. You can't see an assumption but you can see what it does. An assumption is like the foundation of a house: you can't see it but you know it's there and you know the house would fall down without it.

An assumption is something you accept as true to get on with the argument. You accept that "something" as true rather than require its proof.

Assumptions have negative connotations, but to assume something is not necessarily bad. Indeed, every argument has to assume *something*. No argument would ever finish if every little detail had to be proven. Of course, the more assumptions an argument makes, or the more dubious those assumptions, the shakier the argument.

Although assumptions are unstated, the following methods will help you uncover them.

How to Uncover Assumptions

1. **Work backward from the conclusion.** Find the choice that makes the conclusion more likely to be true. If more than one choice supports the conclusion, pick the choice that does so most directly. In this respect, assumptions are just like premises.

2. **Be reasonable.** You assume something because it is reasonable to assume it. If an assumption were unreasonable, the author would be forced to prove it. So any unreasonable choice is incorrect.

3. **Look for the doubtful.** An assumption *cannot* be a trivially obvious truth, otherwise it would be not an assumption but a fact.

4. **Avoid direct quotations.** Since an assumption is unstated, it will not use direct quotations from the argument.

5. **Consider the reasoning.** The type of assumption may vary with the type of argument. In a statistical argument, for example, the author might assume that a certain sample is representative.

Putting the Strategy to Work: Sample Argument No. 3

Questions 1–2

Michael Jackson drinks Pepsi. Since you want to be cool, you should drink Pepsi, too.

1. Which of the following statements are premises of the author's argument?

   I. Michael Jackson drinks Pepsi.
   II. You want to be cool.
   III. You should drink Pepsi.

   (A) I only
   (B) II only
   (C) III only
   (D) I and II only
   (E) I, II, and III

2. Which of the following premises must be included in the author's argument for the conclusion to be considered logical?

   I. Michael Jackson is cool.
   II. Being cool is desirable.
   III. To be cool, you must do what other cool people do.

   (A) I only
   (B) II only
   (C) I and II only
   (D) I and III only
   (E) I, II, and III

Cracking Sample Argument No. 3: Step 1

Question 1 is a *Find-the-Premise* question. Question 2 is a *Supply-a-Premise* question. Supplying a missing premise, of course, is the same thing as supplying an assumption. To answer both questions, remember the premises of an argument—stated and unstated—support the conclusion.

Cracking Sample Argument No. 3: Steps 2 & 3

The first step, as usual, is to isolate the conclusion. What is the author trying to convince us of? Is he trying to convince us that Michael Jackson drinks Pepsi, that we want to be cool, or that we should drink Pepsi?

The author is clearly trying to convince us that we should drink Pepsi. Now that we have the conclusion, the other statements must be the premises!

Cracking Sample Argument No. 3: Step 4

This argument is so clear that we don't need to make a diagram in order to understand it. The author's reasoning is deductive.

Cracking Sample Argument No. 3: Step 5

Question 1: Option III is the conclusion, options I and II are the premises. Choice (D) is the answer.

Question 2: To answer this question, we must find statements that support the conclusion. Remember: Premises are statements that support the conclusion. The correct options, then, will be those choices that make us want to drink Pepsi.

Option I is necessary to the argument. If Michael Jackson were not cool, why should we give a hoot whether he's drinking Pepsi? Option I is true. Eliminate choice (B).

Option II is unnecessary. Even if being cool were undesirable, the argument's explicit premise is that we want to be cool. Option II is false. Eliminate choices (C) and (E).

Option III is necessary, too. Eliminate choice (A) and mark choice (D).

Putting the Strategy to Work: Sample Argument No. 4

1. Some people fear that our first extraterrestrial visitors will not be the friendly aliens envisaged on numerous episodes of *Star Trek*, but rather hostile invaders bent on global dictatorship. This fear is groundless. Any alien civilization that can send emissaries across vast interstellar distances must have acquired the wisdom to control war or it would have destroyed itself long before contacting us.

   The author bases the argument above on which of the following assumptions?

   (A) Our planet will be contacted by extraterrestrial visitors.
   (B) Any civilization capable of interstellar travel has acquired the technology to dominate our planet.
   (C) Any civilization that has learned to control war is also peaceful.
   (D) Alien civilizations are wiser than those on earth.

(E) If an alien civilization were capable of destroying our
planet, it would be useless to resist.

Cracking Sample Argument No. 4: Step 1

This is a *Supply-a-Premise/Assumption* question. We'll use the approach we used in question 2 from Sample Argument No. 3.

Cracking Sample Argument No. 4: Steps 2 & 3

The author is arguing that we should not be frightened of extraterrestrial visitors. The author's conclusion is that any such visitors would not be hostile, having learned to control war. This argument is fallacious, but that needn't concern us. We're looking for a choice that supports the author's claim.

Cracking Sample Argument No. 4: Step 4

This argument is fairly simple, so we'll skip diagramming. We note that the author's reasoning is deductive. We will consider deductive reasoning shortly.

Cracking Sample Argument No. 4: Step 5

(A) This choice does not directly support the author's claim. Whether we have been visited by aliens is irrelevant to whether or not they are friendly. Eliminate.

(B) If anything, this choice is an argument against the author's conclusion. We're looking for a reason to believe that alien visitors will not dominate our planet. Eliminate.

(C) This choice is the answer. Note that there have been civilizations that have controlled war by the use of force. The Roman Empire, for example, enjoyed centuries of peace, punctuated by only minor skirmishes with their conquered barbarians.

(D) See our analysis of choice (A). Eliminate.

(E) See our analysis of choice (B). Eliminate.

A Brief Digression on Counter-Premises

The author supports his claim with premises. The author of an argument sometimes raises a *counter-premise*. A *counter-premise* is a concession to a position with which the author does not completely agree. If the author is arguing in favor of lower taxes, for example, he may admit that lower taxes may hurt certain segments of the population. This admission is a counter-premise because it is a reason against the author's position. The author will go on, of course, to advance more compelling reasons in favor of his position.

How to Find Counter-Premises

1. **Work backward from the conclusion.** Once you've isolated the conclusion, ask whether the statement makes the conclusion less likely to be true. If so, the statement is a *counter-premise.*

2. **Look for counter-premise signal words.** The presence of a counter-premise is frequently revealed by signal words. A partial list of counter-premise signal words includes

but	nevertheless
although	notwithstanding
however	despite
except	nonetheless

Does this list look familiar? It should—these are *trigger words.*

Beware!—if the argument began with conventional wisdom, the trigger word will introduce the *author*'s position. So read carefully. A trigger word indicates the *presence* of a counter-premise, not its location.

The Parts of an Argument: The Reasoning

The way the premises of an argument combine to support the conclusion is known as the *reasoning.* Reasoning is not true or false. Reasoning is either *valid* or *invalid.* If the premises provide sufficient ground for the conclusion, we say that the reasoning is valid, or logical. If the premises are insufficient, we say that the argument is invalid, or illogical. **Note that an argument can have true premises but illogical reasoning, or false premises and logical reasoning.**

The two primary forms of reasoning are deductive and inductive. We will now examine each.

Deductive Reasoning

Logical deduction asks, *If these premises are true, what conclusions must be true?* The epitome of deductive reasoning is the categorical *syllogism:*

premise: All dudes are mortal.
premise: Aristotle is a dude.
conclusion: Therefore Aristotle is mortal.

There are other types of syllogisms:

premise: Either you are male or female.
premise: You are not male.
conclusion: Therefore you are female.

premise: If you eat a lot, you will gain weight.
premise: You eat a lot.
conclusion: Therefore you will gain weight.

premise: History should be preserved.

premise: This is a historical building.

conclusion: Therefore this building should be preserved.

Deductive arguments are not limited to syllogisms. In fact, the classic syllogism (two premises, one conclusion) rarely appears. You often find arguments with three or four premises on the LSAT. We call these *list of premises* arguments, and we will discuss them shortly.

The key point is that in a deductive argument, the conclusion necessarily follows from the premises. If the premises are true, the conclusion *cannot* be false.

Deductive Fallacies

Many deductive fallacies come from unwittingly using language like some sort of mathematical equation. In math, to say that $x = y$ means that $y = x$. Language, however, is not so symmetrical. To say that all communists are socialists does not imply that all socialists are communists, although many students trip into this error. You can't flip-flop sentences like that.

Other deductive fallacies arise from false assumptions hidden in our casual use of everyday language. All of us are more or less sloppy in our use of language. Unfortunately, this often leads to sloppy thinking. Most of us have become accustomed to casually using very simple English phrases (*if/then, either/or, all/some*) that have *very specific* logical meaning consequences.

The purpose of the following drill is to alert you to the dangers lurking in even the most simple statements. (Note: You will probably not see LSAT questions in this format.)

The Slippery English Language: A Drill

Each of the statements below is followed by four choices. Decide whether each choice must be true, could be true, or cannot be true. For the purposes of this drill, base your analysis on logical—rather than factual—considerations only. Remember our maxim: **When in doubt, take each word *literally*. Beware especially of the subtle difference between what *must* be true, and what *could* be true; between what a statement says or *asserts*, and what it merely *suggests*.**

1. Premise: *All penguins have good manners.*

   What can we conclude about each of the following statements?
   (A) All well-mannered animals are penguins.
   (B) Any ill-mannered animal is not a penguin.
   (C) Some well-mannered animals are penguins.
   (D) All animals which are not penguins are ill-mannered.

Analysis:

(A) This does not follow, but it could be true.

(B) This follows; it must be true.

(C) This follows; it must be true. Perhaps *all* well-mannered animals are penguins, but we know at least that some well-mannered animals are penguins.

(D) This does not follow, but it could be true.

2. Premise: *Some tibbits are purple.*

What can we conclude about each of the following statements?
(A) All tibbits are purple.
(B) Some tibbits are not purple.
(C) Some purple beings are tibbits.
(D) All purple beings are tibbits.

Analysis:

(A) This does not follow, but it could be true. This would not be the case if the premise had read: *Only some tibbits are purple.*

(B) This does not follow, but it could be true.

(C) This follows; it must be true.

(D) This does not follow, but it could be true.

3. Premise: *If it rains, the parade is off.*

What can we conclude about each of the following statements?
(A) If it's sunny, the parade is on.
(B) If the parade is off, it rained.
(C) If the parade is on, it did not rain.

Analysis:

(A) This does not follow, but it could be true. Compare the premise to this slight amendment: *Only if it rains is the parade off.* In that case (A) must be true.

(B) This does not follow, but it could be true. See our previous analysis.

(C) This must be true.

(Note: The word unless continues to vex logicians and philosophers. Consider the following statement: *The parade is on unless it rains.* The *safest* way to interpret the word unless is to translate it by substituting the words *if . . . not.* The statement then becomes: *The parade is on if it does not rain.*)

4. Premise: *Either your mother moves out or I do.*

What can we conclude about each of the following statements?
(A) If your mother moves out, I will move out.
(B) If your mother moves out, I will stay.

(C) If your mother does not move out, I will move out.

(D) If your mother does not move out, I will stay.

Analysis:

(A) This does not follow, but it could be true. Perhaps your mother and I will both move out. Either/or statements trouble some students, who wrongly assume that either/or excludes both. It doesn't. (To say this you must do so explicitly: *Either chocolate or vanilla but not both*.)

(B) This does not follow, but it could be true. See our previous analysis.

(C) This must be true.

(D) This cannot be true.

(Note: Some either/or statements *are* mutually exclusive. Consider, for example, *Your first child will be either a boy or a girl*. You can be sure that your child cannot be both. As question 4 demonstrates, some either-or statements are not mutually exclusive. Take, for example, the statement *I will take either French or Spanish this semester*. You know that you will take French or Spanish, but you might take both.)

What About Other Deductive Fallacies?

Aristotle categorized all human knowledge, and while he was at it he cataloged every conceivable logical fallacy. Logical textbooks always include this kind of list.

Such a comprehensive list is pointless for LSAT purposes. The question itself and the answer choices will describe any fallacy you need to know about. The most important deductive fallacies were illustrated in the previous drill. We will consider *inductive* fallacies shortly.

Using Deduction on a List of Premises

The classic example of a deductive argument is the *syllogism*. We gave you some examples of syllogisms earlier. Strictly speaking, a syllogism has two premises and one conclusion (All rabbits are carnivorous; Peter is a rabbit; therefore Peter is carnivorous). A syllogism has three categories, or terms (rabbits, carnivores, and Peter).

The LSAT rarely includes syllogisms. LSAT arguments usually have more than three terms. We call such arguments *All-Some-Most* questions. In them you are given a list of statements, or premises, and a question that asks what you can deduce from those premises.

Putting the Strategy to Work: Sample Argument No. 5

1. All lawyers are businessmen.
    No altruists are politicians.
    Some businessmen are altruists.
    Some politicians are lawyers.

    If the statements above are true, which of the following
    must be true?

    I.   Some lawyers are altruists.
    II. Some politicians are businessmen.
    III. Some businessmen are not politicians.

    (A) I only
    (B) II only
    (C) III only
    (D) I and II only
    (E) II and III only

Cracking Sample Argument No. 5: Step 1

An *All-Some-Most* question in *Triple True/False* format.

Cracking Sample Argument No. 5: Steps 2 & 3

The argument provides us with premises; the question asks us to supply a
conclusion.

Cracking Sample Argument No. 5: Step 4

To organize all the terms and show their relations, we'll use an arrow diagram.

The premises describe different groups of persons and the relations
among them. First, let's see which groups we're working with: lawyers, businessmen, altruists, and politicians—four groups in all.

Arrange these groups in a circle, representing each with a letter or abbreviation:

B

L   A

P

To diagram the first premise, draw an arrow from L pointing to B. Put an *a* above the arrow to indicate "all":

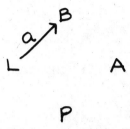

To diagram the second premise, draw an arrow from A pointing to P. Put an *n* above the arrow to indicate "no":

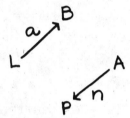

To diagram the third premise, draw an arrow from B pointing to A. Put an *s* above the arrow to indicate "some":

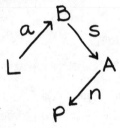

To diagram the fourth premise, draw an arrow from P pointing to L. Put an *s* above the arrow to indicate "some." Here's what your completed diagram should look like:

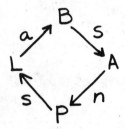

The diagram shows only what you know is true and what you know is not true. **Anything that does not contradict the diagram is permitted.** We know, for example, that some of the businessmen are altruists. Possibly *all* of them are, we don't know.

Cracking Sample Argument No. 5: Step 5

Option I: The diagram shows that all lawyers are businessmen and that some businessmen are altruists. Does this mean that some lawyers must be altruists? No! This is somewhat tricky, but perhaps the businessmen who are altruists are the non-lawyers. This option could be true, but not necessarily. Option I is false. Eliminate choices (A) and (D).

Option II: The diagram indicates that this option must be true. Eliminate choice (C).

Option III: The diagram indicates that some businessmen are altruists. Since any businessman who is an altruist is not a politician, this option must be true. Mark choice (E).

Forget Venn Diagrams

If you learned how to do Venn diagrams in your high-school math class, you know that they can be used to analyze a simple *All-Some-Most* question. Unfortunately, Venn diagrams are cumbersome and don't work at all on longer *All-Some-Most* questions.

Use our arrow diagram.

Inductive Reasoning

Logical induction asks, *If these premises are true, what other conclusions are more or less probable?* Most of your thinking about the world, and certainly all your habits, is based on *inductive reasoning*. An induction is a generalization from limited experience. Inductive reasoning goes *beyond* the premises.

In an inductive argument, an author predicts that a conclusion will be true because similar statements are true, or have been true in the past. In other words, an inductive conclusion does not necessarily follow from the premises. Unlike a deductive conclusion, an inductive conclusion cannot be certain.

The three inductive arguments you need to know are argument by *statistics* (sample), *causal argument* (explanation), and argument by *analogy*. Because inductive arguments go beyond the premises, inductive fallacies are quite common. Let's take a look at each type of inductive argument and its most important fallacies.

Statistical Arguments

Statistical arguments are easy to spot since they use statistics or samples.

> premise: Three out of four lawyers interviewed believe they are under-
> paid.
> conclusion: Of *all* lawyers, *probably* three out of four believe they are
> underpaid.
>
> (unstated premise:) This sample is representative.

(Note the unstated premise/assumption: We cannot be absolutely sure of this conclusion.)

The real world makes it impractical, if not impossible, to test every single instance, so we must rely on samples. For example, every ten years the country gets around to taking a census, but otherwise it relies on samples and polls. The Gallup people evidently have it down to a science, claiming to get a *representative* sample of 250 million people by polling several thousand.

Statistical Fallacies

The most important statistical fallacy is assuming that the sample is representative. That is, assuming that the sample is unbiased.

Causal Arguments

An argument uses premises to show that a conclusion is true. An *explanation* uses factors to make a conclusion understandable. To explain something is to show what caused it.

> premise: Every time X occurs, Y has been observed to follow.
> premise: Every time X does not occur, Y has not been observed to follow.
> conclusion: X *probably* causes Y.
>
> (unstated premises:) Nothing else causes Y.
> We have observed all X's and Y's.

(Note the unstated premises/assumptions: We cannot be absolutely sure of this conclusion.)

An explanation that involves an argument uses causal reasoning. (By the way, we have used this term numerous times already and we trust you have read it correctly—that's *causal* reasoning, not *casual* reasoning!)

How do you spot a causal argument? The wording is generally a clue. Consider the following phrases:

responsible for	gives rise to
owing to	produces
causes	a factor of
needs	brings about
necessary for	leads to
creates	a result of
attributable to	an effect of

You get the idea. Such words and phrases suggest a cause-effect argument. No big deal. LSAT explanations are short; you will have little trouble spotting them.

Causal Fallacies

Causal arguments, like all inductive arguments, are fraught with fallacies. The three most important are:

• failing to consider *alternative causes:*

Let's say that a forest fire occurs. That does not mean someone was careless. There are alternative explanations, like lightning.

• assuming that X caused Y simply because X preceded Y:

Just because a forest fire occurred immediately after you had a picnic in the forest does not mean that you caused the forest fire. Something else might have caused it. Like lightning.

• failing to distinguish between *necessary* and *sufficient:*

A match is sufficient to start a forest fire, but it is not necessary to start a forest fire. Lightning can also start a forest fire.

Arguments by Analogy

Analogies are critical to legal reasoning. Indeed, our very concept of justice assumes that like cases should be treated alike.
Analogies are easy to spot:

premise: Overcrowding of rats leads to aberrant behavior.
conclusion: Overcrowding of people *probably* leads to aberrant behavior.

(unstated premise:)   Human social behavior is similar to that of rats.

(Note the unstated premise/assumption: We cannot be absolutely sure of this conclusion.)

In them one thing will be compared to another, so the wording is a tip-off. The following words and phrases suggest that an analogy is being developed:

> also
> similar
> too
> like
> just as
> compared to

You get the idea. More subtle analogies can be detected when the argument suddenly introduces an object that had not been previously discussed.

All arguments by analogy *assume* that if two things are *relevantly* similar, they will behave similarly, or should be treated similarly. Clearly the primary subject and the analogue have relevant differences as well. That is why, for example, we are more willing to experiment on rats than on people. Arguments by analogy assume that the relevant similarities outweigh any differences.

Fallacies with Analogies

We hinted at the fallacies with analogies in the preceding discussion. The two things being compared may not have relevant similarities, or they may have relevant differences. To return to our sample argument by analogy, rats are probably more physiologically than socially similar to human beings. That does not seem to stop psychology students from putting the tiny critters in mazes, but even they will admit certain behavioral differences.

Even with relevant similarities, the analogy may overlook significant differences. Remember: An analogy can never *prove* an argument, it can only support one.

Always Identify the Type of Reasoning

You now know the difference between a deductive argument and the various kinds of inductive argument. When reading an argument, note the type of reasoning involved. Knowing what kind of reasoning an author is using allows you to anticipate the argument's structure and its possible fallacies.

Putting the Strategy to Work: Sample Argument No. 6

1. A full moon is known to cause strange behavior in people. People are behaving strangely today, so there is probably a full moon.

   Which of the following most closely parallels the kind of reasoning used in the argument above?

(A) Abnormal sunspot activity causes animals to act strangely. We are experiencing abnormal sunspot activity today, so animals are probably acting strangely.

(B) Medical reference books often have red covers. This book has a red cover, so it is probably a medical reference work.

(C) The law of gravity has worked for as long as mankind has been able to observe it. It's working today, and it will probably continue to work tomorrow.

(D) A mental illness has much in common with a physical illness. Therefore mental illnesses should probably be treated in much the same way as physical illnesses.

(E) People with an ear for music often have an equal facility for learning languages. Bill has an ear for music, so he probably has a facility for learning languages.

Cracking Sample Argument No. 6: Step 1

This *Reproduce-the-Reasoning* question asks you to recognize the logical structure of one argument in a different context. In other words, you must use the same reasoning with different premises. The answer will have the same logical form, *even if that form is invalid*. **The answer to this type of question is almost always in a completely different context from that of the original argument.**

Cracking Sample Argument No. 6: Steps 2 & 3

On this type of short-argument question, the conclusion and premises are relatively apparent. The conclusion is tipped off by the signal word "so": *There is probably a full moon.* Everything else constitutes the premises.

Cracking Sample Argument No. 6: Step 4

Stripped down to its essentials, you find the following argument:

Cause (full moon) leads to usual effect (strange behavior);
We find the usual effect (strange behavior);
Therefore, we can conclude cause (full moon).

This flawed *causal* argument ignores alternative causes. Many things other than the full moon can cause strange behavior (Mardi Gras, Halloween, St. Patrick's Day). You are not, however, asked to criticize the argument. In fact, you must find a similarly flawed argument.

Grammatical clues often help to answer this type of question, but diagraming works particularly well.

$$f.m. \rightarrow s.b.$$
$$s.b., \therefore f.m.$$

The power of this approach is that it eliminates the verbiage and allows you to see the underlying structure of the argument. Let's go to the choices:

Cracking Sample Argument No. 6: Step 5

(A) Cause (unusual sunspot activity) leads to effect (strange animal behavior). Cause, therefore effect. This is not the same form as the original argument, although it does bear a seductive surface similarity. Eliminate.

(B) "Cause" (medical reference book) leads to "effect" (red cover). Effect, therefore cause. We used quotation marks to indicate that medical textbooks do not "cause" red covers. We are using the terms loosely, but this argument has the same structure as—and completely different context from—that of our original argument. Bingo. This is the answer unless one of the other choices is better, so we'd better check 'em out.

(C) This argument boils down to the inductive argument that things have been this way in the past, so they'll continue to be this way in the future. This structure is completely different. Eliminate.

(D) This is an argument by analogy. Eliminate.

(E) This choice has the same structure as the argument in choice (A). Eliminate.

Putting the Strategy to Work: Sample Argument No. 7

Questions 1–2

Fortunately for the development of astronomy, observations of Mars were not too exact in Kepler's time. If they had been, Kepler might not have "discovered" that the planets move in elliptical rather than circular orbits, and he would not have formulated his three laws of planetary motion. There are those who complain that the science of economics is inexact, that economic theories neglect certain details. That is their merit. Theories in economics, like those in astronomy, must be allowed some imprecision.

1. The author of the argument above depends upon which of
    the following in reaching his conclusion?

    (A) finding an exception to a general rule
    (B) drawing an analogy
    (C) appealing to an authority
    (D) attributing an unknown cause to a known effect
    (E) using the word "theory" ambiguously

2. A logical critique of the argument above would most
    likely emphasize that the author

    (A) fails to cite other authorities
    (B) does not consider nonscientific theories
    (C) neglects the possibility that there may have been
        other reasons for Kepler's success
    (D) assumes the truth of the very proposition he is trying
        to prove
    (E) ignores the differences between the sort of
        imprecision allowed in astronomy and that allowed
        in economics

Cracking Sample Argument No. 7: Step 1

The first question is a *Classify-the-Reasoning* question, while the second is a
Criticize-the-Reasoning question.

Criticize-the-Reasoning questions are similar to *Weaken-the-Conclusion*
questions in that both weaken the author's argument. The difference between
these two question types is that to criticize the reasoning, you find fault with the
reasoning rather than with the premises (and assumptions). To weaken the conclusion, you find fault with the premises (and assumptions) rather than with the
reasoning.

Cracking Sample Argument No. 7: Steps 2, 3, & 4

These steps are straightforward. All we have to do is recognize the type of
reasoning. Our criticism of that reasoning follows from its type.

The author's conclusion is in the last sentence: *We cannot expect economic theories to be precise.* How does the author support this conclusion? By
pointing out the advantages of imprecision to Kepler's theory in astronomy.

It isn't a sample. It isn't an explanation. It's an analogy.

Cracking Sample Argument No. 7: Step 5

Question 1: Choice (B) is the answer. Choice (C) is superficially plausible,
but the author is not appealing to Kepler as an authority. The other choices are
not defensible.

Question 2: Now that we know we're dealing with an analogy, we can anticipate the stock flaw: overlooking relevant differences between the primary subject and the analogue. Choice (E) is the answer. Choices (A) and (B) might have been relevant if the author's argument had been statistical. Choice (C) is a shot, but the author's argument does not depend on this point. **An argument by analogy depends on there being a relevant similarity between two different objects; it does not depend on their being a complete similarity.** Indeed, an analogy assumes that the two objects being compared are similar despite their differences.

Putting the Strategy to Work: Sample Argument No. 8

1. A psychologist once performed the following experiment. Subjects were divided into two groups: excellent chess players and beginning chess players. Each group was exposed to a position arising from an actual game. Not surprisingly, when asked to reconstruct the position from memory an hour later, the expert chess players did much better than the beginners. On a board where the pieces were placed in a position at random, however, the expert players were no better able to reconstruct the position from memory than were the beginners.

   Which of the following explains the result of the psychologist's experiment above?

   (A) Memory is an important part of chess-playing ability.
   (B) The beginning chess players as well as the experts were less able to memorize the random position than the "actual" position.
   (C) The ability to memorize varies with experience and ability.
   (D) Memory is a skill that can be improved with practice.
   (E) Being able to make sense of information plays an important role in memorization.

Cracking Sample Argument No. 8: Step 1

An *explanation,* like an argument, tries to convince you of something. The difference is that an argument tries to make you accept something, whereas an explanation tries to make you *understand* something.

Cracking Sample Argument No. 8: Steps 2, 3, & 4

This passage asks for an explanation of an experiment's results. There are no conclusions or premises to be analyzed.

To explain something is to show what caused it. Here we are looking for an explanation for different degrees of success in remembering chess pieces. **Don't try to think of your own explanation. Just apply *POE* to the choices.**

Cracking Sample Argument No. 8: Step 5

(A) This is true, but it does not account for why the experts did relatively poorly on the random position. Eliminate.

(B) Again, this does not account for why the expert chess players did worse. Eliminate.

(C) This is true, but it does not explain the outcome. Eliminate.

(D) Again true, but not an explanation. Eliminate.

(E) This is the answer, and would clearly account for the different outcomes.

How to Approach the Section: Pacing

As with the other LSAT sections, you have 35 minutes for this section. That works out to a minute and a half for each question.

As you know, the first step in the Reading Passages section is getting an overview. With the Arguments sections, however, this is unnecessary. Ordinarily you survey a section to decide which *group* of questions you want to avoid. The Arguments sections, however, are the only ones on the LSAT that are not broken down into groups of questions. The questions may progress in some rough order of difficulty.

As always, of course, avoid the format questions when short of time. In general, the shorter the argument, or the choices of the argument, the easier the question. Other things being equal, go for the argument with more than one question—you'll get more bang for your buck.

Common Mistakes

Most students spend too little time analyzing the easy and medium questions, only to spend far too much time agonizing over difficult choices. When analyzing an argument, typical students usually have no trouble eliminating two or three choices quickly. They narrow their selection down to two or three choices. At that point, they cannot decide which choice is *best*. Instead of circling the question and moving on immediately, they struggle to make a decision. They become confused. Then, in desperation, they choose the choice that *seems* best, usually for all the wrong reasons.

Slow down. Get the decision down to two or three choices, then move on to the next question. The longer you spend on the hard choice, the greater your confusion will become. The greater your confusion, the greater your frustration. You vacillate between the choices, and you probably fall for a trap.

Return to the hard choice later, in the final minutes of the section. Then you will not have the time to vacillate. Time pressure will make you more ruthless, and you will be forced to rely on our *POE* guidelines.

Guessing Strategy

The same guessing rules on reading passages apply to arguments. We'll repeat them here. On argument questions:

- Longer choices have an edge over shorter choices—**when, and only when, all *POE* attempts fail, favor the longest choice.** (Don't bother counting words, just eyeball the choices.)
- On *Triple True/False* questions, all three options are usually NOT correct —**when, and only when, all *POE* attempts fail, avoid I, II, and III.**
- The central letters (choices B, C, and D) have a slight edge over the extreme letters (choices A and E)—**when, and only when, all *POE* attempts fail, guess "toward" choices (C) and (D).**
- Three letters "in a row" are not that rare, but you'll almost never find four —**when, and only when, all *POE* attempts fail, avoid a letter if it would create four in a row.** If you're absolutely sure that questions 17, 18, and 19 are (D), (D), and (D), the odds are *overwhelmingly* against question 20's being a (D).

Although these biases are significant, they should *not* override *POE* considerations. **These rules should be used *only* when all else fails—that is, when your 35 minutes are just about up and you're scrambling to fill in any remaining questions you *absolutely* couldn't decide using *POE* or didn't get to.**

Sometimes you find yourself with only seconds to go and, say, half a dozen unanswered questions. If so, use the following rule: **Scan your answer sheet for that section's column and in the remaining blanks, fill in *the* letter that's appeared the least on the questions you've already answered, giving slight priority to choices (C) and (D). There is also the chance the test writers will catch on to these biases and eliminate them.**

This last resort guessing rule is fail-safe. It will work even if the test writers catch on to the biases we just mentioned and randomize the answer choices and characteristics.

Summary

1. Each of the two Arguments section consists of roughly 20 minipassages, called *arguments,* and approximately 25 questions based on them. They are the most important question types on the LSAT.

2. The Arguments sections require no background in formal logic.

3. An *argument* is simply a claim or *conclusion* supported by reasons, or *premises.* An unstated premise is called an *assumption.* The conclusion itself is not always stated.

4. The reasoning of the argument is the way the premises support the conclusion. The two primary forms of reasoning are *deductive* and *inductive*. The sort of reasoning required on the LSAT is pretty basic.

5. Many LSAT arguments contain statements that neither support the conclusion nor raise objections to it. Don't let this other stuff get in your way.

6. To analyze an argument, find its conclusion first. Now that you have the conclusion, find the supporting premises. If necessary, reduce the main idea of the argument to a diagram—this often helps you to understand it. Don't let your diagraming consume a lot of time. Note the type of reasoning. Then go to the choices.

7. To find the conclusion, check the first and last sentences of the argument. If it is not there, check for conclusion signal words. These two techniques will help you locate most conclusions.

8. To find a premise, work backward from the conclusion: The premise will support the conclusion—that is, make it more likely to be true. Look out for any premise words.

9. The author sometimes includes counter-premises. The presence of counter-premises is usually tipped off by *trigger words*.

10. Read the question (not the choices) before you read the argument. Analyze only as much of the argument as you need to answer the question.

11. Two or more choices will often seem plausible. Use *POE*. If you're still stuck, move on to the next question! Return to the question at the end if you have any time left.

12. Arguments are similar to reading passages, but approaches differ in key respects as you can see in the following chart:

Arguments versus Reading Passages: The Major Differences	
Reading Passages	**Arguments**
Primary difficulty: Extracting the answers from a mass of details.	Primary difficulty: Deciding which choice is best from two or three seemingly plausible choices.
How to read: Stick with the first and last sentence of each paragraph, skimming over the details.	How to read: Carefully.
Do not read the questions before the passage unless short of time.	Read the question before the argument.
First step: Get a section overview to decide which passage to sacrifice.	No need for overview. When short of time, skip the longer arguments.

The answers to passage questions often paraphrase the text. A paraphrase choice has a significant edge over a direct quotation choice.	The scope of the argument limits the amount of paraphrasing. Other things being equal, the paraphrase choice has only a slight edge over any direct quotation choice.
The answers tend to be general.	The scope of the argument limits how general the answer can be. Traps tend to generalize beyond the scope of the argument.
The answers tend to be indisputable.	The answer to many types of argument questions *cannot* be indisputable.

13. The conclusion of a deductive argument follows *necessarily* from its premises. By contrast, the conclusion of an inductive argument follows more or less *probably* from its premises. The three types of inductive arguments you must know are *statistical arguments, arguments by analogy,* and *explanations.*

14. To solve an *All-Some-Most* question, use an arrow diagram.

15. Almost all LSAT argument questions can be classified under one of the following headings:

- *Find-the-Conclusion/Supply-a-Conclusion/Weaken-(Strengthen)-the-Conclusion*
- *Find-the-Premises/Supply-a-Premise (find an assumption)*
- *Classify-the-Reasoning/Reproduce-the-Reasoning/Criticize-the-Reasoning*

16. If you're almost out of time, fill in all remaining blanks by guessing B, C, or D, whichever has appeared least on the questions you've completed.

CHAPTER 5

Games

The Games section contains four sets, or games. Each game includes 5 to 7 questions, so the section totals 22 to 24 questions.

Before we begin, take a moment to read the instructions to this section:

> Directions: Each group of questions is based on a set of conditions. In answering some of the questions it may be useful to draw a rough diagram. Choose the best answer for each question and blacken the corresponding space on your answer sheet.

These are the directions that will appear on your LSAT. As usual on the LSAT, the official directions are very little help. Review them now. They will not change. Don't waste time and points reading them in the test room.

CRACKING THE SYSTEM: THE LSAT

The Good News

Of the LSAT sections, Games terrifies test takers the most. Games are unlike anything you've ever seen on a standardized test. No single method handles every type of game. No college course prepares you for this section, although math helps somewhat. Practice makes perfect, but improvement comes slowly. All but the very strong test takers must resign themselves to sacrificing one set completely.

But do not give up the ship.

All Is Not Lost

First everyone's in the same boat. Games may be new to you, but they are less difficult than they used to be.

While there is no single way to solve all games, we do have a general strategy and a group of techniques to help you handle virtually every type of game you can expect.

Don't get hung up on games. Treat them as puzzles.

As Usual, Consider Omitting Part of the Section

Almost all students would improve their score on the Games section by omitting an entire game. Unless you are shooting for one of the very highest LSAT scores, count on not completing this section. Even if you're an ace at games, you should save the hardest games and hardest questions for last.

If you sacrifice one game, you'll have approximately two minutes per question on the remaining sets. That should be enough time to work out the questions carefully. Careless misreading is the most common source of errors in the Games section.

Trust us: The hardest game simply isn't worth attempting unless you are quite good at games (for example, you make at most one mistake on any of the sample games in this chapter).

What Is a Game?

Games are mind benders. Each game consists of a number of *elements* in an initial situation that we call the *setup*. This situation is incompletely described in a set of conditions or *clues*. Sometimes these clues are modified by a question. If so, the new clues apply to that question only.

Your job is to play Sherlock Holmes by drawing conclusions based on those clues to answer questions.

What Does This Section Test?

Games test how well you can organize an incomplete set of indirect clues so that you can extract information quickly.

Why Is This Section on the LSAT?

It beats us. Games test your ability to determine various sorts of spatial relationships. It bears no relation to anything lawyers do.

How to Crack Games

The directions say that rough diagrams may help you solve some of the questions. This recommendation is misleading—diagrams are *the* way to solve games.

We will teach you the most important diagrams. Some students think they can solve games without diagrams. Sure they can—at home. Don't kid yourself by thinking you can solve games without diagrams in the pressure of the actual exam room.

How Many Types of Games Appear?

Surprisingly few.

We will give you a representative game for those games that have appeared most frequently on recent LSATs. Once you master the themes and techniques to solve our representative games, you should be able to handle any game on the LSAT.

As we go to press, we can say with some assurance that the most common games on recent LSATs are typified by our Sample Games numbers 1 and 4. See also our Games Drill questions numbers 1, 2, 4, 6, 14, 16, and 19.

No Quick Fix to Games

No single diagram or method works on all games. We can, however, teach you a handful of approaches that will help you in most situations. Even if you already do well on this section, our techniques can make your life easier.

The more experience you have solving games, the better. Nothing beats practice. If you haven't already bought a volume of real LSATs—the more recent the better—you should do so immediately.

What You Will See

Let's start off with an easy sample game that has one illustrative question. (We will present this game with all of its questions shortly.) Work it out on your own before reading the analysis that follows.

Mr. Andersen, irascible head of the Evanston Cub Scout
Troop, is assessing the trustworthiness of his six young

charges. Mr. Andersen has reached the following preliminary conclusions:

> Alvin is more trustworthy than Brent.
> Frederick is not more trustworthy than Edwin.
> Brent is more trustworthy than Cecil.
> Dave is less trustworthy than Edwin.

5. Which of the following is a possible order of the six cubs described in the passage above, from most trustworthy to least trustworthy?

(A) Edwin, Alvin, Frederick, Brent, Dave, Cecil
(B) Alvin, Edwin, Cecil, Dave, Brent, Frederick
(C) Frederick, Alvin, Edwin, Brent, Dave, Cecil
(D) Dave, Alvin, Edwin, Brent, Frederick, Cecil
(E) Frederick, Brent, Dave, Alvin, Edwin, Cecil

Here's how to crack it: Each game usually has one question that can be done without a diagram. Always do such a question first. Simply match each condition, or clue, against the choices.

Some students apply all of the clues to the first choice, then all of the clues to the second choice, and so on. Such a procedure is inefficient. **To use _POE_ efficiently, work _exclusively_ with the most specific or definite clue first.** Apply that one clue to all the choices. Eliminate as many choices as you can. Then apply the next definite clue to the remaining choices, and so on.

The first clue contradicts choice (E). Eliminate (E). The second clue contradicts (C). Eliminate (C). The third clue contradicts choice (B). Eliminate (B). The second clue contradicts choice (D). Eliminate (D). Only one choice remains. Mark choice (A).

On this question we needed all of the clues, but quite often you find the answer before using the last clue. Remember: **Apply the easiest clue to all of the choices before you move on to the second clue.**

How You Will Improve Your Games Score

If you apply yourself diligently, you will learn how to

1. recognize the most common games
2. use powerful methods of diagraming to solve any game
3. develop an intuitive feel for games
4. improve your score by working out _fewer_ questions
5. save time by doing the questions in a certain order

Practice, Practice, Practice

We can show you how to do games, but the only way for you to feel comfortable with them is to practice.

Do games over and over during spare moments. They are more fun than crossword puzzles. Do a game one way, then try it another way. Put the game aside for a week and try it yet another way. Slowly but surely our methods will become instinctive.

Beware: **Practicing games in a leisurely way at home is *much* easier than doing them under time pressure in the actual exam room.** Far too many students look at games a couple of weeks before the LSAT and, after tinkering with an easy question or two, say to themselves, "This section doesn't look too bad. No problem."

Watch out. We suggest that you time yourself when you do a game—no more than two minutes a question—and then review the game afterward at your leisure.

How to Read This Chapter

Work through this chapter at least twice. Play with the games on your first run. Get a feel for different approaches. You have a lot to grapple with, so absorb the techniques gradually. Do not try to remember things; with practice our techniques will become routine.

Our General Step-by-Step Strategy for Solving Games

We said earlier that we don't have a single approach that works for all games. That's true, but we do have a general strategy. This strategy spells out the basic steps you'll take in approaching each game.

Here are the basic steps in our general strategy.

Step 1: Read the setup and get the big picture.
Step 2: Draw a diagram and symbolize the clues.
Step 3: Decide question order.
Step 4: Use efficient *POE* to attack the questions.

Before we discuss these steps we'll give you a sample game to work out on your own. This is the same game we saw earlier with all of its questions. After you have completed the questions, our analysis will illustrate the application of each of these steps.

Sample Game No. 1: Rankings

Mr. Andersen, irascible head of the Evanston Cub Scout Troop, is assessing the trustworthiness of his six young charges. Mr. Anderson has reached the following preliminary conclusions:

Alvin is more trustworthy than Brent.

Frederick is not more trustworthy than Edwin.

Brent is more trustworthy than Cecil.
Dave is less trustworthy than Edwin.

1. How many cubs must be more trustworthy than Cecil?

   (A) 5
   (B) 4
   (C) 3
   (D) 2
   (E) 1

2. What is the maximum number of cubs who could be more trustworthy than Frederick and less trustworthy than Cecil?

   (A) 4
   (B) 3
   (C) 2
   (D) 1
   (E) 0

3. If a seventh cub, Geoff, is more trustworthy than exactly four of the six cubs described in the passage above, which of the following must be true?

   (A) If Alvin is more trustworthy than Geoff, Geoff is less trustworthy than Cecil.
   (B) If Cecil is more trustworthy than Edwin, Geoff is more trustworthy than Cecil.
   (C) If Frederick is less trustworthy than Dave, Geoff is more trustworthy than either Alvin or Edwin.
   (D) If Frederick is more trustworthy than Cecil, Geoff is less trustworthy than either Frederick or Cecil.
   (E) If Brent is more trustworthy than Dave, Geoff is more trustworthy than Edwin.

4. Which of the following statements could be true?

   I. Alvin is more trustworthy than Frederick, but less trustworthy than Edwin.
   II. Exactly three cubs are more trustworthy, and one cub less trustworthy, than Edwin.
   III. Cecil and Dave are equally trustworthy.

   (A) I only
   (B) II only
   (C) III only

(D) I and II only

(E) I, II, and III

5. Which of the following is a possible order of the six cubs described in the passage above, from most trustworthy to least trustworthy?

(A) Edwin, Alvin, Frederick, Brent, Dave, Cecil
(B) Alvin, Edwin, Cecil, Dave, Brent, Frederick
(C) Frederick, Alvin, Edwin, Brent, Dave, Cecil
(D) Dave, Alvin, Edwin, Brent, Frederick, Cecil
(E) Frederick, Brent, Dave, Alvin, Edwin, Cecil

6. Which of the following is a complete and accurate list of the six cubs described in the passage above who could be least trustworthy?

(A) Cecil
(B) Cecil, Dave
(C) Cecil, Dave, Edwin
(D) Cecil, Dave, Frederick
(E) Cecil, Dave, Edwin, Frederick

7. If Brent and Dave are equally trustworthy, which of the following must be true?

   I. At least four cubs are more trustworthy than Cecil.
   II. At least two cubs are more trustworthy than Dave.
   III. At least three cubs are less trustworthy than Alvin.

(A) I only
(B) II only
(C) II only
(D) I and II only
(E) I, II, and III

Cracking Sample Game No. 1: Step 1 (Getting the Big Picture)

This game doesn't look that bad. There are only six elements (cubs) and four clues, so we have plenty of information to go on. The questions look okay, with only one format question and one question that changes the initial clues.

Cracking Sample Game No. 1: Step 2 (Draw the Diagram)

We want to start with the most specific or concrete clue. Only the second clue seems a little vague, so we'll start with the first. Here's what we drew:

A
B

You'll notice that we used a letter to represent each name. The test writers are usually nice enough to give you elements that begin with different letters so you don't get confused. We like to indicate relative sizes by placing one element above or below another.

There are other ways to diagram this clue. Here's one:

A > B

Here the clues go from left to right. Someone else might have drawn them from right to left. Which symbol you use is largely a matter of preference, so long as you are consistent. We will discuss symbols at length in our drill.

Now we need to *link* the first clue to another, ideally one that contains Alvin or Brent—the third.

A
B
C

It's a good idea to cross off clues as you diagram them so that you don't overlook any. Anyway, since we don't have any other clues to link to these two, we'll look for another definite clue—the fourth.

A   E
B   D
C

We had to separate the two columns of letters to indicate their independence. We can draw conclusions only within a column. Both Dave and Edwin, for example, could be more trustworthy than Alvin, although our diagram suggests they are both less trustworthy. We'll have to keep in mind that each letter is free to move up or down in the diagram, but not sideways.

We can link the final clue—the second one provided—to the third as follows:

A
B E F
C D

The dotted line indicates a "ceiling": F (Frederick) can be anywhere (be more or less trustworthy than anyone) so long as he isn't above (more trustworthy than) E (Edwin).

That's our completed diagram.

Cracking Sample Game No. 1: Step 3 (Decide Question Order)

Question 5 is the easiest, as we noted at the beginning of this chapter. We're looking for *must* questions and questions that provide additional clues; we're avoiding format questions and those that change the initial clues.

Here is an efficient question order:

Question 5 (simple matching of clues against choices)
Question 1 (*must* question)
Question 2 (*could* question)
Question 6 (*could* question)
Question 7 (*must* question, *Triple True/False* format)
Question 4 (*could* question, *Triple True/False* format)
Question 3 (alters the original setup)

Cracking Sample Game No. 1: Step 4 (Use Efficient *POE*)

We've already done question 5. Back to question 1.

1. How many cubs must be more trustworthy than Cecil?

    (A) 5
    (B) 4
    (C) 3
    (D) 2
    (E) 1

Here's how to crack it: A *must* question. Our diagram indicates that only Alvin and Brent must be more trustworthy than Cecil. Dave, Edwin, and Frederick *could* be more trustworthy, but don't have to be. The answer is choice (D). If you misread this as a *could* question, you probably guessed choice (A).

2. What is the maximum number of cubs who could be more trustworthy than Frederick and less trustworthy than Cecil?

    (A) 4
    (B) 3
    (C) 2
    (D) 1
    (E) 0

Here's how to crack it: A *could* question. We're looking first for those cubs who could be more trustworthy than Frederick, but also less trustworthy than Cecil. Since Cecil is linked to more cubs than is Frederick, let's look first for those less trustworthy than Cecil. Only Dave, Edwin, and Frederick can be less trustworthy. Of those, nothing prevents Dave and Edwin from being more trustworthy than Frederick.

If you sketched this out next to your original diagram, your work so far should look something like this:

6. Which of the following is a complete and accurate list of the six cubs described in the passage above who could be least trustworthy?

    (A) Cecil
    (B) Cecil, Dave
    (C) Cecil, Dave, Edwin,
    (D) Cecil, Dave, Frederick,
    (E) Cecil, Dave, Edwin, Frederick

Here's how to crack it: A *could* question. Since we want to use efficient *POE*, we look first to the initial clues. Our initial diagram tells us that Alvin, Brent, and Edwin cannot be least trustworthy. We can eliminate any choices that contain these cubs: (C) and (E).

Again using efficient *POE,* we glance over our analysis of earlier questions for any insights we can apply here. Our analysis of question 2 revealed that F could be the least trustworthy. The answer must contain Frederick, so we eliminate choices (A) and (B). Mark choice (D).

7. If Brent and Dave are equally trustworthy, which of the following must be true?

    I.   At least four cubs are more trustworthy than Cecil
    II. At least two cubs are more trustworthy than Dave.
    III. At least three cubs are less trustworthy than Alvin.

    (A) I only
    (B) II only
    (C) III only

(D) I and II only

(E) I, II, and III

Here's how to crack it: A *Triple True/False must* question that provides an additional clue. A little time-consuming, but otherwise no problem for efficient *POE*.

Let's incorporate the new info linking Brent and Dave into our diagram. Here's what your updated worksheet should look like:

Now let's go through the options. Which option do we start with? Always start with the easiest option. Here the options look equally difficult, so let's just crank through them in order.

Option I: Our diagram indicates that Alvin, Brent, Cecil, and Dave must be more trustworthy than Edwin. Option I is true, which allows us to eliminate choices (B) and (C).

Option II: Our diagram indicates that Alvin and Edwin must be more trustworthy than Dave. Option II is true. Eliminate choice (A).

Option III: Our diagram indicates that Brent, Cecil, and Dave must be less trustworthy than Alvin. Option III is true. Mark choice (E).

4. Which of the following statements could be true?

   I. Alvin is more trustworthy than Frederick, but less trustworthy than Edwin.

   II. Exactly three cubs are more trustworthy, and one cub less trustworthy, than Edwin.

   III. Cecil and Dave are equally trustworthy.

   (A) I only

   (B) II only

   (C) III only

   (D) I and II only

   (E) I, II, and III

Here's how to crack it: A *Triple True/False could* question. Remember: **Always glance over your analyses of previous questions for a headstart on the current question.** In this case, option III can exploit the insights gained in solving question 4. We know that Brent and Dave can be equally trustworthy.

Can Cecil and Dave? Sure, the original clues do not prohibit this. Here's one possible ordering, updating our worksheet:

Option III could be true. Using *POE* efficiently, we eliminate all choices that do not include this option: (A), (B), and (D).

Two options and two choices remain. Which option should we check next? The easier option, of course. How clever we were, the work we did for option III (see previous diagram) confirms option I. Option I could be true.

Only one choice includes options I and III; mark choice (E). Once again we see how efficient *POE* allows us to sidestep analyzing an option.

3. If a seventh cub, Geoff, is more trustworthy than exactly four of the six cubs described in the passage above, which of the following must be true?

    (A) If Alvin is more trustworthy than Geoff, Geoff is less trustworthy than Cecil.
    (B) If Cecil is more trustworthy than Edwin, Geoff is more trustworthy than Cecil.
    (C) If Frederick is less trustworthy than Dave, Geoff is more trustworthy than either Alvin or Edwin.
    (D) If Frederick is more trustworthy than Cecil, Geoff is less trustworthy than either Frederick or Cecil.
    (E) If Brent is more trustworthy than Dave, Geoff is more trustworthy than Edwin.

Here's how to crack it: A *must* question, but one that alters the original conditions. Actually, this question adds another element (another cub) without substantially altering the original clues as embodied in our basic diagram.

Anyway, Geoff is more trustworthy than four of the six cubs. Looked at from the other side, Geoff is *less* trustworthy than—or equally as trustworthy as—two of the original cubs. We have numerous possibilities for who these two cubs might be: Alvin and Brent, Alvin and Edwin, Dave and Edwin, and Edwin and Frederick. And for each of these possibilities, we have several possible orderings of the four cubs who are less trustworthy than Geoff.

Whew! Where do we start? Whenever you are presented with the prospect of numerous possibilities, never write them all out. Instead, go immediately to the choices and apply *POE*.

Which choice do we start with? Since no choice seems any easier than the others, we'll go through them alphabetically.

(A) A little fiddling shows that this is not necessarily true. Eliminate choice (A). Here's our worksheet so far:

(B) If Cecil is more trustworthy than Edwin, we can link five of the six cubs as follows:

F (Frederick) can go anywhere, but wherever he goes, G (Geoff) must remain more trustworthy than C (Cecil). This choice must be true. Mark choice (B). We'll stop our analysis here since we never want to do more work than necessary to answer a question.

That completes our analysis of Sample Game No. 1.

Now that you've seen the general strategy applied to a sample game, let's explore the steps in detail.

Step 1: Read the Setup and Get the Big Picture

Most students rush right in and start diagraming before they've read the entire setup. Relax. Pause for a few seconds before you start your diagram and get the big picture.

Here are the factors you should consider:

• **How familiar is this game?** Obviously the more familiar the game is, the more quickly you can move through it. If you've never seen the game before, perhaps you should skip it.

• **How many questions are in this set? What types of questions are they?** The more questions, the more time you can afford to invest in the initial diagram. Why? Because you can apply your insights to getting more answers. The time-consuming part of most games is setting up the initial diagram. Once you have the initial diagram and a couple of insights, the questions can be solved rather quickly.

Another consideration is the types of questions. Certain types of questions require special handling. We will discuss this shortly.

• **How many clues does the setup provide?** All games are more or less incomplete: The clues do not allow you to reconstruct the situation completely. You might think that a lot of clues increases your work. This is not true. Each clue decreases the amount of thinking you must do. If you were a detective, would you want a lot of clues or a few? A lot, obviously. The more clues a setup provides, the easier the game. If a game has only a few clues and a lot of elements, anything's possible, so don't waste too much time trying to draw conclusions; you don't have much to go on. Sketch a rough diagram and get to the questions. The more clues you have, the more time you should spend on the initial diagram.

Step 2: Draw a Diagram and Symbolize the Clues

As we said before, diagraming is the key to this section: Make a good diagram and you're almost home free; make a bad diagram and you're lost. What you want is a diagram that will organize the clues efficiently. We will show you the most important types of diagrams shortly.

The key word at this point is *quickly*. You have less than two minutes a question. If you cannot decide which diagram applies, skip the set and do an easier one. If this *is* the easiest set, put down *something*. Start symbolizing the clues. Do not waste time trying to be clever. Get to the questions! Fiddling with the clues and the information provided in the questions often reveals the key to the game. **If you can't figure out a good diagram, don't waste time: Fiddle with the clues to answer the questions!**

Consider Drawing the Initial Diagram in Pen

Most questions provide clues that modify the initial diagram. **If a question modifies the initial setup, it does so for that question only.** Once you leave that question, you must return to your original diagram and start all over.

Because of this, many students prefer to draw the initial diagram with the pen provided for the writing sample and do later analysis in pencil. Having the initial diagram in pen helps them remember which clues were provided in the initial setup and which clues pertain to one question only.

Some students find this step awkward. It's no big deal whether you use a pen or not, but you must remember not to modify your original diagram beyond recognition.

When *Not* to Diagram

Should you always diagram a game? No, not *always*. We solved the first question in this chapter simply by matching each clue against the choices. If you're running short of time, don't waste it by beginning to diagram a new game. Almost every game has a question or two that can be answered without resorting to a diagram.

Having said that, we strongly recommend that in all other cases you use a diagram.

Read Each Clue Carefully!

A single overlooked word can cause you to botch every question in a game unwittingly! Consider the subtle but critical difference in wording between *Noah and Mary cannot play on the same team* and *Noah and Mary cannot play in the same game*. In the first instance they could play in the same game if they played on opposing teams. This is a good time to review our comments in the previous chapter under *Deductive Fallacies* and The Slippery English Language (page 65).

Designing Effective Symbols

A symbol is more than a shorthand expression. A good symbol will help you think; a bad symbol will confuse you. A symbol represents something. Your symbol must clearly represent what you want it to represent, and nothing else. Ideally your symbol should represent as much information as possible, without suggesting unintended assumptions.

Choosing the right symbol is an art. Your symbol for something may be different from our symbol for something. If your symbol packs in as much information as our symbol does—fine, use it. Still, you should experiment with different symbols to see what works best for you.

The following drill will give you a chance to do just that. What your symbols reveal about your thinking may surprise you. We'll work through the first few examples with you. But try them on your own before reading our analysis.

Games Drill: Symbols

Directions: For each of the following words or phrases, construct a symbol. If more than one symbol occurs to you, use each of them. Try to incorporate any further conclusions suggested by the limited information provided. (Note: We realize that this drill is somewhat artificial since an appropriate symbol often depends on the major diagram being used.)

Clue	Symbol(s)
1. In a line, B is between A and C.	

Analysis: A lot of students use the following faulty symbol: ABC

Can you see what's wrong? It assumes alphabetical order! A better symbol would be something along the following lines:

This symbol incorporates the information without assuming anything.

2. Camilla will play only if Louise plays.	

Analysis: Many students use the following symbol: $\boxed{CL}$

Another popular symbol is this $L \to C$

Both symbols are faulty since each assumes that if Louise plays, Camilla will play. We cannot assume this. We know that if Camilla is playing, Louise must also be playing. We know nothing about the *flip-flop* situation. Camilla plays only if Louise plays, but if Louise plays we don't know that Camilla is playing. A better symbol would be something like this: $C \to L$

3. Four girls and three boys stand in row.	

Analysis: The symbol $4g, 3b$ is inadequate since it merely repeats the information in shorthand. Remember: **A good symbol should represent the information as literally as possible.** As much as time and efficiency permit, represent each element with its own symbol. Something along the following lines would be better:

$$gggg\,bbb\,\_\,\_\,\_\,\_\,\_\,\_\,\_$$

Of course, if the information had said 14 boys and 13 girls, you'd have to adopt some sort of abbreviation since writing our 27 letters would consume too much time.

4. In a six-story hotel, J lives two floors above K.	

Analysis: Many students botch this by assuming that two floors separate J and K. J lives two floors above K, so only *one* floor separates them. If we use a dash to indicate "not," here is what your diagram should look like:

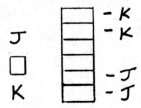

Notice the additional conclusions we have incorporated.

Okay, now you're on your own. The complete analysis of this drill is at the end of the chapter.

5. At least one adult must accompany each child.	
6. If Bill plays first, Tom plays second.	
7. A bag contains ten marbles: yellow, blue, and green. The number of blue marbles does not exceed the number of yellow marbles.	
8. Some boys study French.	
9. Of the three boxes, two are red.	
10. Tom and George never work together.	
11. A, B, and C are juniors; D, E, and F are seniors.	
12. Mr. and Mrs. Smith and their two children, Terry and George	
13. Five adjacent two-story houses	
14. In a sprint, W finishes before X, X finishes before Y, and Z finishes before Y.	
15. Point A is four inches from Point B, and Point B is two inches from Point C.	

16. A certain shelf has three French books, two Spanish books, and four German books. The French books are next to each other. The Spanish books are not next to each other.	
17. All students enrolled in chemistry are also enrolled in physics. Each student enrolled in physics is enrolled in either philosophy or music, but not both.	
18. Towns P, Q, R, and S are connected to each other by the following roads: R is connected to P and Q only; S is connected to Q only; P is connected to R and Q only.	
19. Five graduate students—J, K, L, M and N—are seated at a round table. L does not sit next to J. K sits next to N.	
20. All blue cars are convertibles. The first car is a convertible.	

When *Not* to Symbolize

Ideally, you should symbolize every clue. Some clues, however, are difficult to symbolize, especially negative clues that do not refer to any specific element. For example, consider the following clues:

- No more than three books of the same subject are put on the shelf.
- Players cannot score more than three points in the first round.

These clues cannot be symbolized in any convenient fashion. The key word, as always, is *quickly*. If you cannot think of a way to symbolize a clue, put an asterisk next to it and return to it when solving the questions.

Symbolize the Most Concrete Clue First

We've spoken about symbolizing the clues, but not about the order in which you should approach them. **Read through all the clues before you symbolize any particular one.** The clues are in no particular order, and you must often link two or more clues sequentially. Look for the clue that gives you something specific to work with, and start symbolizing there.

Next Look for a Clue to *Link* to the First

For example, suppose your first clue in the Games sample question we gave you earlier told you that Alvin is more trustworthy than Brent. The ideal next clue would be one mentioning either Alvin or Brent. In that way you could link the two clues and perhaps draw some conclusions.

After you've linked the first two clues, look for a clue to link to the second, and so on. You won't always be able to do this, but look for the opportunity whenever possible.

Check Off Clues as You Go

It's all too easy to overlook a clue *entirely*. Check off each clue as you incorporate it into your diagram. As we suggested earlier, put an asterisk next to any clue for which you can't devise a symbol.

Once You've Finished Your Diagram, Get to the Questions

Don't spend too much time contemplating your completed diagram before attacking the questions. Doing so wastes time. And the more time you spend *thinking* and not *doing*, the more likely you are to go astray.

Step 3: Decide Question Order

Game questions are in no particular order. As always, you want to do the easy ones first and save the harder ones for later. Here are our guidelines:

• **Do *must* questions before *could* question.** A *must* question means that it is possible to determine the answer directly. A *could* question means that you might have to do a lot of fiddling. Generally speaking, *could* questions are more difficult than *most* questions. We will discuss *must* versus *could* questions next under *POE*.

• **Do questions that provide additional clues before questions without clues.** Remember Sherlock: The more clues you have, the less thinking you have to do. Let's say you're a detective on a robbery case. An eye witness describes the robber as being tall and in his mid-30s. Initially that's all you have to go on. If the next day another witness tells you that the robber has green eyes, you have more information to work with. Your job is that much easier. The same is true of questions that provide new clues.

• **Format questions can be tricky or time-consuming or both.** Put these off as long as possible.

• **Do questions that *alter* the initial clues *last*.** Some questions provide additional clues. These questions tend to be easy. Some questions *alter* the original clues. These clues tend to be hard since you have to redraw the initial diagram to comply with the changed conditions.

To return to our previous example, if the first eye witness recants and says that the robber was not in his mid-30s but in his mid-60s, you're going to have to start your search from scratch.

If You Get Stuck on a Question, Skip it!

This will probably happen to you on the actual LSAT, and probably more than once. If it does don't panic, and don't waste time. Skip the question and try easier ones in the set. Often doing a different question reveals the key to unlocking a more difficult question.

Step 4: Use Efficient *POE* to Attack the Questions

You want to do as little work and thinking as possible; just enough to answer the question. The following guidelines will help you with an efficient *POE:*

• **Apply one clue to all the choices before applying the second clue.** We saw an example of this method in the first question in this chapter.

• **Eliminate as many choices as possible from the setup before you analyze any new clues.** Each new clue helps, but sometimes the new clue is unnecessary. Use every opportunity to save time!

• **Check out your work on any previous questions—sometimes you can carry over earlier conclusions.** Because you can carry over conclusions: **Never erase any of your work!**

• **Keep your eye on the choices *as you solve the question.*** You will occasionally solve a question without realizing it if you ignore the choices. This trap is especially true of *could* questions.

Using *POE* on *Must* Questions

We implied earlier that a *must* question can usually be solved by "logic," whereas a *could* question often involves fiddling. If you cannot figure out a *must* question, do not waste time with logic—try any choice! Fiddle. If that choice works, eliminate any other choice that does not agree with it. Then try one of the remaining choices.

To show you what we mean, let's consider the following example. You don't need to see the game to which it refers:

1. If a female serves as club president in 1985, in which of the following years must a male serve as secretary?

   (A) 1984
   (B) 1985
   (C) 1986

(D) 1984 and 1985

(E) 1985 and 1986

For illustrative purposes, let's say that you couldn't figure this question out entirely but you had fiddled with it and deduced that a male *could* serve in 1984. Which choices can you eliminate?

Here's how to crack it: This is a *must* question, but we know that a male *could* serve in 1984. If a male could serve in 1984, then the answer must include at least 1984. You can rule out any choice that omits 1984. Eliminate choices (B), (C), and (E). Only two choices remain. The answer is either 1984 only, or 1984 and 1985.

That is all you can conclude with the limited information we have provided. If we gave you more information, you would fiddle with 1985 to see if it works.

Putting the Strategy to Work: Major Types of Games

The most common games on recent LSATs are *Rankings*, *Family Trees*, *Maps*, and *Things-in-a-Line*. You've already worked through an example of the first. You are about to work through the others.

These names are our titles; they will not be labeled as such on your test. Some games on the LSATs will clearly fit into one of these categories. The classification of other games will be less obvious. **You must learn to recognize the type of game you are dealing with, since your approach will vary from one type to another.** After giving you a chance to solve these games on your own, we will give you what we consider to be the most appropriate diagram for each. If you can't decide what sort of game you're dealing with, skip it! If not, fiddle with the questions. Don't think, fiddle!

Work each one out on your own before reading the analysis that follows. Time yourself: two minutes per question!

Sample Game No. 2: *Family Tree*

A genealogist has completed a study of the Clampett family and drawn the following conclusions:

Carla Jo has only one daughter, Audry, and only one granddaughter, Dot.

Billy Bob has exactly two grandsons, one of whom is Fletcher.

Hank is the only child of Dot and the only grandson of Audry.

Everett has one sister, Audry, and one brother, Billy Bob. Irene is Billy Bob's daughter-in-law and Fletcher's mother.

Kev is the nephew of Irene's husband and the son of
   Garrett.
Jed is Audry's son-in-law.
No children have been born out of wedlock, no family
   member has been married more than once, and no
   blood relative has married any other.

1. Everett's sister-in-law is Fletcher's

    (A) aunt
    (B) great-aunt
    (C) second cousin
    (D) paternal grandmother
    (E) maternal grandmother

2. If Everett is married to Lulu, Lulu is

    (A) Dot's aunt
    (B) Irene's blood relative
    (C) Hank's grandmother
    (D) Kev's mother
    (E) Garrett's grandmother

3. Garrett is Fletcher's

    (A) cousin
    (B) father
    (C) father-in-law
    (D) grandfather
    (E) uncle

4. Jed is Hank's

    (A) cousin
    (B) brother-in-law
    (C) father
    (D) grandfather
    (E) great-grandfather

5. Which of the following must be true?

    (A) Garrett's wife is Audry's daughter
    (B) Irene's husband is Hank's grandfather
    (C) Billy Bob's wife is Hank's grandmother
    (D) Audry's husband is Kev's nephew
    (E) Carla Jo's husband is Garrett's grandfather

6. Which of the following could be the brother-in-law of Garrett's wife?

    (A) Irene's husband
    (B) Audry's husband
    (C) Dot's father
    (D) Hank
    (E) Fletcher

7. If Billy Bob is married to Myrtle, Myrtle is

    (A) Jed's blood relative
    (B) Hank's grandmother
    (C) Kev's grandmother
    (D) Irene's blood relative
    (E) Carla Jo's blood relative

Cracking Sample Game No. 2: Step 1

Family Tree games can get a little complicated with three or four generations, but answering the questions is quite easy once you've drawn your initial diagram. Although the Games section is not supposed to require any specific knowledge, you'd better know your family relationships if you want to do well on *Family Tree* games. These games have appeared frequently enough in the past couple of years that it will probably pay to spend a few minutes reviewing the difference between a cousin and a second cousin, for example, or that between a great aunt and a maternal grandmother.

In any event, this game and its questions don't seem too bad.

Cracking Sample Game No. 2: Step 2

The first clue seems specific enough. Here's how we'd begin our diagram:

Circles for females, squares for males (and triangles for persons of unknown gender) are standard family tree symbols. You might have indicated husbands for Carla Jo and Audry with blank squares (since we don't know their names), but there's no need to jump the gun. Their husbands might be divorced or deceased.

The asterisk—since we can't think of any convenient way to symbolize this—reminds us that Dot is Carla Jo's *only* granddaughter and Audry's *only* daughter.

Now we want a clue to link to Carla Jo, Audry, or Dot. How about the third? The asterisk reminds us that Hank is Audry's only only grandson.

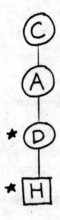

Let's look for the next clue to link to our diagram. The fourth clue looks promising. Here's what your diagram should look like so far:

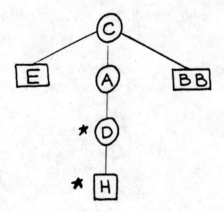

The seventh clue tells us that Audry's son-in-law is Jed. Since Audry has only one daughter, Dot, Jed must be Dot's husband.

Here's what your diagram should look like:

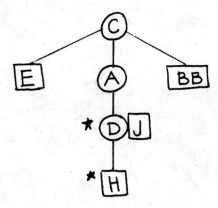

Now, the second clue tells us that Billy Bob has two grandsons, but have you figured out the gender of Billy Bob's child or children yet? Let's say you haven't figured it out. No problem. We don't want to waste time thinking, so let's just put down a triangle (for person of unknown gender). We don't know whether Billy Bob's other grandson is Fletcher's brother, so let's just put a blank square off to the side. Again, we use asterisks to remind us of a clue we haven't been able to symbolize completely.

The fifth clue tells us that Irene is Fletcher's mother and Billy Bob's daughter-in-law. Billy Bob's daughter-in-law must be married to Billy Bob's *son*. Now we certainly realize that the triangle beneath Billy Bob should be a square, indicating a male. (Perhaps you had already cleverly deduced this from the earlier clue that Dot was Carla Jo's only granddaughter—all of Billy Bob's children must be males.)

Anyway, here's our diagram so far:

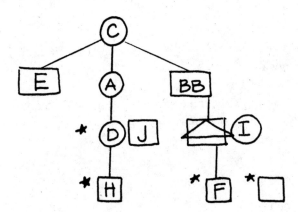

The last clue to incorporate is the sixth. Since Kev is the nephew of Irene's husband (Fletcher's dad), we now know that Kev and Fletcher are cousins.

Here's what our completed diagram looks like:

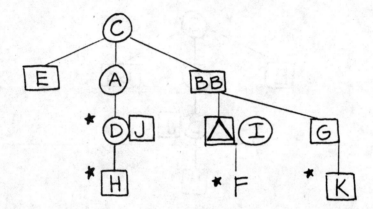

Cracking Sample Game No. 2: Step 3

None of these questions looks especially difficult, but a rough ordering from easiest to hardest is probably, 3, 4, 1, 5, 6, 2, 7.

Cracking Sample Game No. 2: Step 4

Our diagram indicates all of the relationships, so we will provide commentary only when necessary. If the diagram you constructed matches ours, any mistakes you made are probably attributable to misreading a question.

3. Garrett is Fletcher's

(A) cousin
(B) father
(C) father-in-law
(D) grandfather
(E) uncle

Here's how to crack it: A *must* question. Our diagram indicates that choice (E) is the answer. Students who do not read the second, fifth, and sixth clues carefully select choice (B).

4. Jed is Hank's

(A) cousin
(B) brother-in-law

(C) father
(D) grandfather
(E) great-grandfather

Here's how to crack it: A *must* question. Our diagram indicates that choice (C) is the answer.

1. Everett's sister-in-law is Fletcher's

    (A) aunt
    (B) great-aunt
    (C) second cousin
    (D) paternal grandmother
    (E) maternal grandmother

Here's how to crack it: A *must* question. Everett's sister-in-law must be Billy Bob's wife, who is the mother of Fletcher's father. Choice (D) is the answer.

5. Which of the following must be true?

    (A) Garrett's wife is Audry's daughter
    (B) Irene's husband is Hank's grandfather
    (C) Billy Bob's wife is Hank's grandmother
    (D) Audry's husband is Kev's nephew
    (E) Carla Jo's husband is Garrett's grandfather

Here's how to crack it: A *must* question.
(A) The diagram contradicts this choice. Eliminate.
(B) The diagram contradicts this choice. Eliminate.
(C) The diagram contradicts this choice. Eliminate.
(D) The diagram contradicts this choice. Eliminate.
(E) The diagram confirms this choice. Select choice (E).

6. Which of the following could be the brother-in-law of Garrett's wife?

    (A) Irene's husband
    (B) Audry's husband
    (C) Dot's father
    (D) Hank
    (E) Fletcher

Here's how to crack it: A *could* question. Garrett's wife could have brothers-in-law through other family trees, but in the Clampett family tree Irene's husband is the only shot. Choice (A) is the answer.

2. If Everett is married to Lulu, Lulu is

(A) Dot's aunt
(B) Irene's blood relative
(C) Hank's grandmother
(D) Kev's mother
(E) Garrett's grandmother

Here's how to crack it: A *must* question, but one that alters the original conditions. If you want to put Lulu in the diagram next to Everett, feel free. It should be obvious, however, that Everett is Dot's uncle, so his wife would be Dot's aunt. Choice (A) is the answer.

7. If Billy is married to Myrtle, Myrtle is

(A) Jed's blood relative
(B) Hank's grandmother
(C) Kev's grandmother
(D) Irene's blood relative
(E) Carla Jo's blood relative

Here's how to crack it: A *must* question, but, again, one that alters the original conditions. If you match each of the choices against the diagram until you find a match, you will discover that choice (C) is the answer.

Sample Game No. 3: Map

Sparks Pendleton, radar man on the U.S.S. *Waterloo*, has recorded the positions of various planes during training exercises at precisely 14:00.

Plane 1 is northwest of Plane 4 and Plane 7.
Plane 2 and Plane 4 are due south of Plane 3.
Plane 6 is south of Plane 1 and west of Plane 2.
Plane 5 is northeast of Plane 4 and northwest of Plane 7.

1. Plane 7 is currently located in which direction from Plane 6?

(A) north
(B) northwest
(C) east
(D) west
(E) southeast

110

2. Which of the following planes could currently be located due west of Plane 7?

   I. Plane 1
   II. Plane 2
   III. Plane 3

   (A) I only
   (B) II only
   (C) III only
   (D) II and III only
   (E) I, II, and III

3. Plane 5 is currently located in which direction from Plane 1?

   (A) north
   (B) east
   (C) south
   (D) southwest
   (E) northwest

4. What is the minimum number of planes that must currently be located north of Plane 4?

   (A) 0
   (B) 1
   (C) 2
   (D) 3
   (E) 4

5. What is the maximum number of planes that could currently be located due south of Plane 6?

   (A) 0
   (B) 1
   (C) 2
   (D) 3
   (E) 4

6. Which of the following must be true?

   (A) Plane 5 is currently located northeast of Plane 2.
   (B) Plane 4 is currently located northwest of Plane 7.
   (C) Plane 6 is currently located west of Plane 4.
   (D) Plane 1 is currently located east of Plane 3.
   (E) Plane 5 is currently located northeast of Plane 6.

Cracking Sample Game No. 3: Step 1

Map games are never too difficult. This one provides a fair number of clues, and the questions don't look too bad. Sometimes you have to do a little fiddling with your diagram to get all the relative positions straight, but otherwise this type of game isn't tough.

(Note: Those fastidious test writers have slipped up once again. Games are not supposed to require any outside knowledge. For those of you who aren't professional cartographers, the word "due" means *directly.* If you didn't catch the distinction between, say, *north* and *due north,* you probably missed a few questions.)

Cracking Sample Game No. 3: Step 2

The second clue seems the most concrete, so let's start there. On our diagram, we use the top of the page to be north, the bottom to be south, and so on. Since we don't know the relative positions of Planes 2 and 4, we'll have to allow for two possibilities:

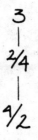

The straight line indicates a due direction; we'll use arrows to represent general directions.

Okay, let's link the first clue to what we have diagramed so far:

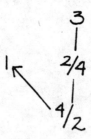

It doesn't matter if the arrow points from Plane 4 to Plane 1 or vice versa. We've omitted Plane 7 since we don't know where it is relative to Plane 4. We'll put Plane 7 down shortly, when we get more info on it.

Another important convention in our diagram: As we've drawn it, Plane 1 is north of Plane 2. This might not be the case. Think of the arrows used in this type of game as extendable or collapsible. Plane 1 can move away from or toward Plane 4.

Okay, let's link the third clue to our diagram:

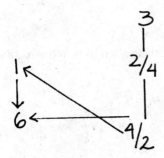

We don't actually know if Plane 6 is north or south of Planes 2 and 4, but we do know it is to the west of both.

The fourth clue tells us where to place Plane 5, and also Plane 7.

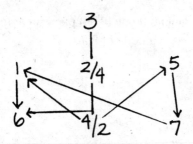

Remember: **The positions indicated are relative, not absolute.** A plane can be anywhere in the diagram so long as its relation to the other planes does not violate any of the clues.

Cracking Sample Game No. 3: Step 3

The most efficient question order is probably 1, 3, 4, 6, 5, 2.

Cracking Sample Game No. 3: Step 4

1. Plane 7 is currently located in which direction from Plane 6?

   (A) north
   (B) northwest
   (C) east
   (D) west
   (E) southeast

Here's how to crack it: A *must* question. Plane 6 is west of Planes 2 and 4, which are west of Plane 5, which is west of Plane 7. So Plane 7 is east of Plane 6. Mark choice (C). If you selected choice (D), perhaps you misread the question. Choice (E) is possible, but we cannot be sure that Plane 7 is south of Plane 6.

3. Plane 5 is currently located in which direction from Plane 1?

    (A) north
    (B) east
    (C) south
    (D) southwest
    (E) northwest

Here's how to crack it: A *must* question. The answer is choice (B), using exactly the same analysis as that used in answering question 1.

4. What is the minimum number of planes that must currently be located north of Plane 4?

    (A) 0
    (B) 1
    (C) 2
    (D) 3
    (E) 4

Here's how to crack it: A *must* question. According to our diagram, Planes 1, 3, and 5 must be located north of Plane 4. Planes 6 and 7 could be, but don't have to be. The answer is choice (D).

6. Which of the following must be true?

    (A) Plane 5 is currently located northeast of Plane 2.
    (B) Plane 4 is currently located northwest of Plane 7.
    (C) Plane 6 is currently located west of Plane 4.
    (D) Plane 1 is currently located east of Plane 3.
    (E) Plane 5 is currently located northeast of Plane 6.

Here's how to crack it: A *must* question.
    (A) This choice could be true, but doesn't have to be. Eliminate.
    (B) Ditto.
    (C) This must be true. This is the answer.
    (D) This cannot be true. Eliminate.
    (E) This could be true, but not necessarily. Eliminate.

5. What is the maximum number of planes that could currently be located due south of Plane 6?

(A) 0
(B) 1
(C) 2
(D) 3
(E) 4

Here's how to crack it: A *could* question. According to our diagram, none of the planes can be located *due* south of Plane 6. The answer is choice (A).

2. Which of the following planes could currently be located due west of Plane 7?

I. Plane 1
II. Plane 2
III. Plane 3

(A) I only
(B) II only
(C) III only
(D) II and III only
(E) I, II, and III

Here's how to crack it: A *Triple True/False could* question.

Option I: This cannot be true, which is evident from our diagram as well as from the first clue. Eliminate choices (A) and (E).

Option II: This could be true. Eliminate choice (C).

Option III: This could be true. Eliminate choice (B). Mark choice (D).

Sample Game No. 4: *Things-in-a-Line*

Dutch O'Dane, mercurial coach of the All-Star Little Leaguers, has decided the first game's batting order of the nine team members–R, S, T, U, V, W, X, Y, and Z. The following conditions refer to the positions in the starting lineup only:

Three people bat between V and W.
S bats immediately before U and immediately after T.
X bats before Y.
R bats fourth.

1. If three times as many players bat before Z as bat after, which of the following must be true?

(A) S bats first.
(B) V bats fifth.
(C) X bats sixth.
(D) Y bats seventh.
(E) W bats eighth.

2. If W bats fifth, which of the following is a complete and accurate list of the positions in which X can bat?

(A) first, second
(B) first, second, third
(C) first, sixth, seventh
(D) first, second, sixth, seventh
(E) first, second, third, sixth, seventh

3. T can bat in which of the following positions?

   I. Fifth
  II. Sixth
 III. Seventh

(A) I only
(B) II only
(C) III only
(D) II and III only
(E) I, II, and III

4. Each of the following is a possible batting order (from first to last) EXCEPT

(A) T, S, U, R, V, X, Y, Z, W
(B) V, X, Y, R, W, T, S, U, Z
(C) W, X, Z, R, V, Y, T, S, U
(D) X, V, Y, R, T, S, U, W, Z
(E) T, S, U, R, W, Z, X, Y, V

5. If R bats fifth but all of the other conditions hold, then V can bat in which of the following positions?

   I. Second
  II. Third
 III. Fourth

(A) I only
(B) II only
(C) III only
(D) I and III only
(E) I, II, and III

6. If X bats third and Y bats fifth, which of the following must be true?

    (A) T bats seventh.
    (B) V bats seventh.
    (C) W bats second.
    (D) V bats first.
    (E) Z bats second.

Cracking Sample Game No. 4: Step 1

Most beginners have trouble with *Things-in-a-Line* games, but the actual diagram is easier than the one for family trees or maps. Learn how to do this type of game; only rarely is it truly difficult.

Having said that, we will admit that this Things-in-a-Line particular game is in fact difficult. How could you have anticipated that? By comparing the number of clues (only four) to the number of elements (nine). **The fewer the clues relative to the number of elements, the more difficult the game.** Why? Because we don't have much information to go on.

Another thing: Remember that a clue is just another word for a condition, restriction, or requirement. This game provides few clues. In other words, this game places few restrictions on its elements. Almost anything goes!

The final complicating factor is that the questions accompanying this game don't look too easy. All things considered, if this game was on your LSAT, you would have postponed it until you'd completed all the easy games.

Cracking Sample Game No. 4: Step 2

Since we have nine positions, let's number them accordingly in our basic diagram:

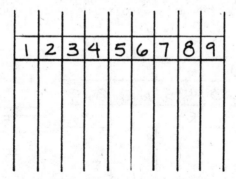

You'll notice that we've left a little space above each position. We've done this to note any clues. We've also left a lot of space below each position so that we can use the same diagram for all of the questions.

Okay, let's start with the most concrete clue—the fourth:

1	2	3	4	5	6	7	8	9
			R					

We've drawn a line under the R to reserve this first row for the initial clues that we're sure about (we'll use the space above the positions to note "negative" clues).

Now let's diagram the second clue:

-S -U	-U						-U	-T -S
1	2	3	4	5	6	7	8	9
			R					

T	S	U

We've put boxes around T, S, and U to indicate that these players bat consecutively. While we're at it, we quickly note what's going on at the extremes: Players T and S cannot be last, nor can players S and U be first.

We indicate these prohibitions with minus signs above the respective positions. Actually, if we gave the matter a little more thought we could deduce other restrictions on T, S, and U. Don't waste your time! Always do as little thinking (and assuming) about the clues as possible. The great danger in thinking too long is introducing faulty assumptions.

We'd better leave this clue and move on to the third one:

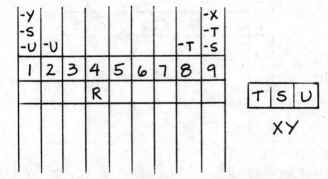

-Y -S -U	-U					-T	-X -T -S	
1	2	3	4	5	6	7	8	9
			R					

T	S	U

X Y

We haven't placed boxes around Players X and Y because they do not necessarily bat consecutively. As with T, S, and U, we noted the restrictions at the extremes.

Here's how we incorporated our final clue, the first:

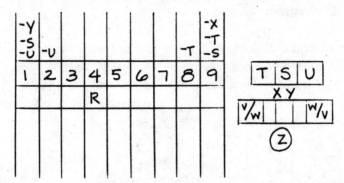

Since we don't know who bats before whom, V or W, we indicated both possibilities.

You notice that we placed Z down with a circle around him. We did so to remind us that Z is a *wild card*. Always note those elements that have no restrictions on them. Such wild cards come in handy when you are working through the questions.

Cracking Sample Game No. 4: Step 3

Question 4 is an *EXCEPT* question, but one that can be done without a diagram. We do these types of questions first. Question 5 alters the initial setup, so we'll do it last. Using our other guidelines for ranking the difficulty of a set's questions, we arrived at the following order: 4, 6, 1, 2, 3, 5.

Cracking Sample Game No. 4: Step 4

4. Each of the following is a possible batting order (from first to last) EXCEPT

   (A) T, S, U, R, V, X, Y, Z, W
   (B) V, X, Y, R, W, T, S, U, Z
   (C) W, X, Z, R, V, Y, T, S, U
   (D) X, V, Y, R, T, S, U, W, Z
   (E) T, S, U, R, W, Z, X, Y, V

Here's how to crack it: An *EXCEPT* question, but one that can be answered by matching the clues against the choices. Choice (D) violates the first clue. Mark choice (D).

6. If X bats third and Y bats fifth, which of the following must be true?

   (A) T bats seventh.
   (B) V bats seventh.
   (C) W bats second.

(D) V bats first.

(E) Z bats second.

Here's how to crack it: A *must* question that provides two additional clues. Remember what we discussed under *POE:* Don't think too long on *must* questions. Just throw anything down that satisfies the conditions and use *POE.*

Let's say we put players T, S, and U in positions 7, 8, and 9. Then we can put players Z, V, and W in positions 1, 2, and 6.

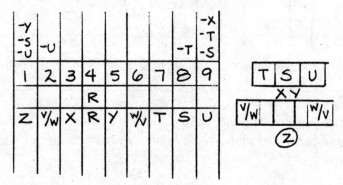

This arrangement is not the only possible one, it is simply the first one that occurred to us. Using *POE,* we can eliminate every choice that contradicts it. If more than one choice remains, we'll throw down another possible arrangement and repeat the process.

(A) This choice is possible. Let's go on to the next choice.

(B) V does not have to bat seventh since he could bat second or sixth. Eliminate.

(C) W does not have to bat second since V does. Eliminate.

(D) V does not have to bat first. Eliminate.

(E) A does not have to bat second since he could bat first. Eliminate.

The first arrangement we came up with by fiddling has eliminated every choice but (A). Mark choice (A).

1. If three times as many players bat before Z as bat after, which of the following must be true?

(A) S bats first.

(B) V bats fifth.

(C) X bats sixth.

(D) Y bats seventh.

(E) W bats eighth.

Here's how to crack it: A *must* question that provides an additional clue, albeit oblique. Before analyzing the additional clue, however, we always check the analyses we've already done to see if we can squeeze out information to apply to the present question. Since our diagram tells us that player S cannot bat first, we eliminate choice (A).

Now, the new clue tells us that six players bat before Z, and two players bat after. Player Z, then, bats seventh. Eliminate choice (D).

Now we'll go to our diagram. If player Z bats seventh, the only available slots for players T, S, and U are positions, 1, 2, and 3. That forces players V and W to positions 5 and 9, though not necessarily respectively. (By now you should have noticed, if you haven't already, that players V and W are interchangeable. Whenever V can bat, W can bat, and vice versa. Whatever could or must be true for one, could or must be true for the other. A standard and powerful technique in this type of game.)

Eliminate choices (B) and (E). Players X and Y must go in slots 6 and 8. Mark choice (C).

2. If W bats fifth, which of the following is a complete and accurate list of the positions in which X can bat?

    (A) first, second
    (B) first, second, third
    (C) first, sixth, seventh
    (D) first, second, sixth, seventh
    (E) first, second, third, sixth, seventh

Here's how to crack it: A *could* question that provides an additional clue. The first thing we notice is that all of the choices include the first position, so we don't need to check that spot. Now, using efficient *POE*, we scan our previous work for something we can exploit here. Sure enough, in our analysis of Question 4 we found acceptable arrangements in choices (B) and (E) where player X batted second and seventh respectively. The answer must contain these two positions. Eliminate choices (A), (B), and (C).

The two remaining choices reveal that player X can bat sixth, so we have to check if he can bat third. Sure, a little fiddling and we come up with the following acceptable sequences:

	1	2	3	4	5	6	7	8	9
-y / -s / -u	-U							-T	-x / -s / -U
				R					
	Z	Y/W	X	R	Y	W/V	T	S	U
	T	S	U	R	Y/W	X	Z	Y	W/V
	V	Z	X	R	W	Y	T	S	U

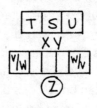

Mark choice (E).

3. T can bat in which of the following positions?

    I. Fifth
    II. Sixth
    III. Seventh

(A) I only
(B) II only
(C) III only
(D) II and III only
(E) I, II, and III

Here's how to crack it: A *Triple True/False could* question. Let's see what previous work we can exploit. Bingo. Our work on question 4 revealed that T can bat first, sixth, and seventh. Options II and III are true. Eliminate choices (A), (B), and (C).

We'll have to check out option I. Let's see if T can bat fifth. If T bats fifth, S and U must bat sixth and seventh. Unfortunately, with R batting fourth, we don't have enough slots for V and W to be separated by three positions.

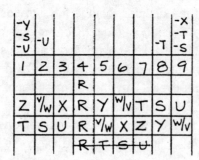

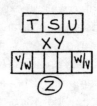

Option I is false. Mark choice (D).

5. If R bats fifth but all of the other conditions hold, then V can bat in which of the following positions?

I. Second
II. Third
III. Fourth

(A) I only
(B) II only
(C) III only
(D) I and III only
(E) I, II, and III

Here's how to crack it: A *Triple True/False could* question that alters the original setup. This question has three strikes against it.

If R now bats fifth, let's change our original diagram.

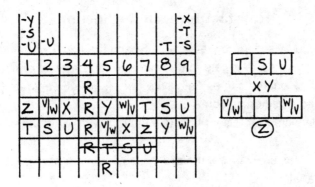

Now we simply check the options using efficient *POE*.

Option I: If V bats second, W would have to be four slots away, or sixth. Fine, no problem. We can toss players T, S, and U into slots 7, 8, and 9. Then let's put X and Y into slots 3 and 4, and *wild card* Z into slot 1.

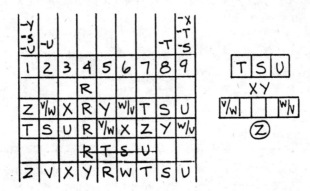

There are, of course, other possible arrangements with V batting second, but this is a *could* question. Option I is true. Eliminate choices (B) and (C).

Option II: If V bats third, W would have to bat seventh. Whoops. We don't have room for players T, S, and U. Option II is false. Eliminate choice (E).

Option III: If V bats fourth, W must bat eighth. Players T, S, and U would have to bat first, second, and third. Fine. Players X and Y can bat sixth and seventh, and *wild card* Z can bat ninth.

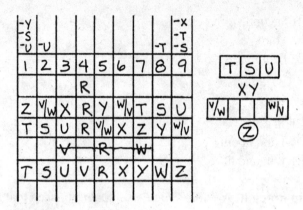

Option III is true. Mark choice (D).

How to Approach the Section

As always, begin by sizing up the section. Spend the first few minutes checking out each of the games. The sets may be in a rough order of difficulty, but you should still check out the games quickly to decide which set to do last. Indeed, you may have to sacrifice an entire set.

To decide which set to sacrifice, use the following guidelines:

- Which game seems most unusual or least familiar or most difficult? Do it last, if at all.
- Which game has the toughest-looking, most time-consuming questions? Do it last.
- Which game has the fewest clues? (The fewer the clues, the more open-ended and difficult the game.) Do it last.
- If the games appear to progress in difficulty, one of the last two games will be the most difficult.

Once you have chosen a game or two to sacrifice, quickly budget your time on the remaining games.

Pacing

You probably will not have enough time to work out all four sets completely, but you should have enough time to work out 2½ or 3 of the 4 sets. Read carefully so that your initial diagram is precise. Once you draw the initial diagram correctly, the only cause of errors is careless rushing. So slow down.

Pacing in the Games section is similar to pacing in the Reading Passages section. You're going to have to leave a game or two out to do your best. It is better to leave out an entire game than to leave out a couple of questions in this game and a couple of questions in that one. Of course, if you're down to the last couple of minutes, you might want to jump to the questions in the last set or two that can be done simply by matching the clues against each of the choices.

A key difference between pacing in Games and in Reading Passages is the amount of time you spend on the questions. With Reading Passages, you cut through the passage relatively quickly so that you can spend most of your time with the questions. The reverse is true with Games. With Games you spend the bulk of your time setting up and analyzing the initial diagram. Armed with an efficient diagram, you'll be able to slice through the questions fairly quickly.

Here's a sample pacing chart:

↓

Time 1:00 section overview (skim all the games; decide which game or games to do last)

↓

Time 12:00 first game (5 minutes on the diagram; 6 minutes on the questions)

↓

Time 23:00 second game (6 minutes on the diagram; 6 minutes on the questions)

↓

Time 35:00 third game (6 minutes on the diagram; 6 minutes on the questions; possibly skip the last couple of long/hard questions here to do the easiest questions in the fourth game; *final seconds fill in all remaining blanks*)

Common Mistakes

The most common mistake is moving too fast—almost all test takers would improve their score by doing *fewer* questions. We've said it before and we'll say it again: For most students, the hardest game just isn't worth attempting. By attempting an impossible game, most students waste time and botch a lot of questions on the easier games that they could have gotten. Better to work out 18 questions and get 16 right than to attempt all 23 and get 14 right.

Guessing Strategy

You will almost certainly not reach 4 to 8 questions in this section. Remember to fill in the blank. Our guessing rules remain pretty much the same. On games questions:

• The central letters (choices B, C, and D) have a slight edge over the extreme letters (choices A and E), and a big edge on questions where all of the choices are numbers arranged by size (from smallest to largest or from largest to smallest)—**when, and only when, all *POE* attempts fail, guess "toward" choice (C) and (D).**
• On Triple True/False questions, all three options are usually NOT correct —**when, and only when, all *POE* attempts fail, avoid I, II, and III.**
• Three letters "in a row" are not that rare, but you'll almost never find four —**when, and only when, all *POE* attempts fail, avoid a letter if it**

would create four in a row. If you're absolutely sure that questions 17, 18, and 19 are (D), (D), and (D), the odds are *overwhelmingly* against question 20 being a (D).

Although these biases are significant, they should *not* override *POE* considerations.

These rules should be used *only* when all else fails—that is, when your 35 minutes is just about up and you're scrambling to fill in any remaining questions you *absolutely* couldn't decide using *POE* or didn't get to. There is also the chance the test writers will catch on to these biases and eliminate them.

Sometimes you find yourself with only seconds to go and, say, half a dozen unanswered questions. If so, use the following rule: **Scan your answer sheet for that section's column and in the remaining blanks, fill in *the* letter that has appeared the least on the questions you've already answered, giving slight priority to choices (C) and (D).**

This last-resort guessing rule is fail-safe. It will work even if the test writers catch on to the biases we just mentioned and randomize the answer choices and characteristics.

Summary

1. The Games section contains 4 sets or games. Each set includes between 5 and 7 questions, so the section includes about 23 questions.

2. Games is the most unusual section on the LSAT. Fortunately, it contains the fewest questions. The only real way to get better at games is to practice.

3. Ideally, you want to get to the point where you approach games questions mechanically. The more mechanical your approach, the less likely you will be to panic on the test.

4. Tackle LSAT games during idle moments as you would crossword puzzles.

5. Most students would improve their Games score by omitting an entire game. Begin the Games section by scanning. If you sacrifice one game, you will have approximately two minutes per question on the remaining sets.

6. Here's our basic, step-by-step strategy for solving a game:
   Step 1: Read the setup and get the big picture.
   Step 2: Draw a diagram and symbolize the clues.
   Step 3: Decide question order.
   Step 4: Use efficient *POE* to attack the questions.

7. When deciding which games you should do, here are the signs you should look for:
   • a type of game with which you are familiar and about which you feel confident
   • a game with a lot of clues

- a game with six or seven questions, which will enable you to make more efficient use of your diagrams
- a game with easy questions
- whether the section seems to progress in difficulty

8. Don't try to do it in your head. Almost all games are best solved by diagrams.

9. Use your writing sample pen to draw your initial diagram and fill in the given clues. That way you can use your pencil to work on individual questions and be able to return quickly to the original setup.

10. Do the easier questions first. Save complex or format questions for last.

11. Don't waste too much time searching for a clever diagram. If you can't figure something out—fiddle!

12. When short of time, look for questions that can be solved by matching clues against the choices.

13. Familiarize yourself with the major types of diagrams.

14. Use our *ACE* guessing rule for any questions you don't get to.

Analysis of the Symbols Drill

The following discussion of the symbols drill will show you what we think are the best symbols to use in each case. If more than one symbol is possible, we'll give you a choice. Quite often several possible symbols will occur to you. Just use the one you feel most comfortable with. We will, however, point out faulty symbols and explain why they are faulty.

Clue	Possible symbols
5. At least one adult must accompany each child.	$C \rightarrow A^+$

Analysis: The symbol CA^+ is faulty. It implies that whenever an adult is present a child accompanies him or her. If you have a child, you must have an adult, but the flip-flop is not necessarily true. See example 2.

6. If Bill plays first, Tom plays second.	$B_1 \rightarrow T_2$

Analysis: As in the previous example, the symbol $B_1 T_2$ is faulty since it implies that Tom's playing second requires Bill to play first. Beware flip-flops.

7. A bag contains ten marbles: yellow, blue, and green. The number of blue marbles does not exceed the number of yellow marbles.	$\{y \geq b; g\} \ 10$ $0 < b < 5$ $0 < g \leq 8$ $0 < y \leq 8$

Analysis: Note the additional conclusions we have drawn. If you didn't deduce all these conclusions, you would have uncovered them through trial and error in answering these questions.

8. Some boys study French.	$b \xrightarrow{s} F$

Analysis: Note: Possibly *all* boys study French, we don't know. All we do know is that at least some of them study French. Some students assume that this clue means, "Some boys study French, *but not all do.*" Beware assumptions, and again, beware flip-flops.

9. Of the three boxes, two are red.	□ □ □ r r ?

Analysis: Again, possibly *all* three boxes are compacts. Some students misread this clue as "Of the three boxes, *only* two are red." (Of course, sometimes the test writers are careless and this is what they intend. If so, it will be apparent from context.) Assume nothing, and read carefully!

10. Tom and George never work together.	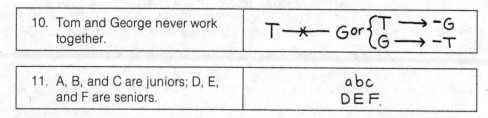

11. A, B, and C are juniors; D, E, and F are seniors.	a b c D E F

Analysis: Uppercase and lowercase letters are useful differentiating symbols.

12. Mr. and Mrs. Smith and their two children, Terry and George	[S]—(S) [G] △T

Analysis: We know the sex of Mr. and Mrs. Smith, and of George, but Terry's gender is unclear. Some students prefer using uppercase and lowercase letters to suggest gender, in which case you'd have something like the above.

13. Five adjacent two-story houses	(grid of five two-story boxes)

14. In a sprint, W finishes before X, X finishes before Y, and Z finishes before Y.	WXY ZY

Analysis: Notice how we have *linked* the first and second clues. **In ranking diagrams like this, be consistent in reading left-to-right or right-to-left.**

| 15. Point A is four inches from Point B, and Point B is two inches from Point C. |  |

Analysis: The dotted lines remind us that we don't know where Points A, B, and C are exactly. Many students assume that Points A, B, and C lie on the same straight road, and they also assume alphabetical order from left to right. Assume nothing! It doesn't matter where you put Point A and Point B, but once you put Point B down, you know that Point C must be somewhere on a two-inch radius.

| 16. A certain shelf has three French books, two Spanish books, and four German books. The French books are next to each other. The Spanish books are not next to each other. | 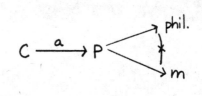 |

Analysis: Don't forget to use a letter to represent each book.

| 17. All students enrolled in chemistry are also enrolled in physics. Each student enrolled in physics is enrolled in either philosophy or music, but not both. | 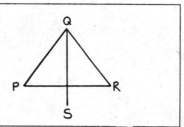 |

| 18. Towns P, Q, R, and S are connected to each other by the following roads: R is connected to P and Q only; S is connected to Q only; P is connected to R and Q only. |
 Q
 P   R
 S |

Analysis: Sometimes questions like this involve one-way roads, so read carefully to see whether or not you must include arrows.

| 19. Five graduate students—J, K, L, M, and N—are seated at a round table. L does not sit next to J. K sits next to N. | 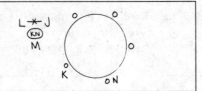 |

Analysis: We can place K and N anywhere, but after that we must place all others in reference to them.

| 20. All blue cars are convertibles. The first car is a convertible. | $B \xrightarrow{a} C.$ $1^{st} = C.$ |

Analysis: Just because the first car is a convertible does not mean that it's blue. Beware flip-flops!

CHAPTER 6

The Writing Sample

The Writing Sample is a 30-minute ungraded essay whose topic is assigned. Your essay is supposed to be an argument supporting either of two given positions. You'll receive a booklet containing both the topic and the space in which to write your essay. You will also receive scratch paper and a special pen. The pen is yours to keep even if you aren't admitted to law school.

Before we begin, take a moment to read the instructions to this section:

General Directions: You are to complete the brief writing exercise on the topic inside. You will have 30 minutes in which to plan and write the exercise. Read the topic carefully. You will probably find it best to spend a few minutes considering the topic and organizing your thoughts before you begin writing. DO NOT WRITE ON A TOPIC OTHER

THAN THE ONE SPECIFIED. WRITING ON A TOPIC OF YOUR OWN CHOICE IS NOT ACCEPTABLE.

There is no "right" or "wrong" answer to this question. Law schools are interested in how carefully you support the position you take and how clearly you express that position. How well you write is much more important than what you write. No special knowledge is required or expected. Law schools are interested in organization, vocabulary, and writing mechanics. They understand the short time available to you and the pressured circumstances under which you will be writing.

Confine your writing to the lined area inside this booklet. Only the blocked lined area will be reproduced for the law schools. You will find that you have enough space in this booklet if you plan your writing carefully, write on every line, avoid wide margins, and keep your handwriting a reasonable size. Be sure your writing is legible.

These are the instructions that will appear on the cover of your LSAT Writing Sample booklet. You'll be given a chance to read them before you write your essay.

The Writing Topic

Inside the booklet you'll find the assigned topic and 50 blank lines on which to write your essay. The assigned topics are so innocuous they're downright dorky. Expect a topic something like this:

Your company, Oh-So-Tight Jeans, has an opening for Director of Marketing. The selection process has narrowed the field down to two candidates. You boss has asked you to prepare a recommendation in favor of hiring one or the other. Since salary requirements are similar, your decision should be guided by two considerations:

• The Director of Marketing should be able to come up with strong, innovative campaigns.
• The Director of Marketing should work well with current Oh-So-Tight Jeans employees, especially the sales force.

Susan Baldwin, 28, graduated #1 in her Harvard Business School class three years ago. She received her MBA in marketing, earning a special commendation for her thesis, "Marketing to the Underclass." Ms. Baldwin's first employer was Natural Baby Foods, where she quickly established herself on the fast track by becoming the youngest product manager in the history of Natural Baby Foods. Known as a savvy number cruncher, Ms. Baldwin is completely versed in all the latest marketing techniques. She does not, however, have any experience in the fast-changing garment business.

Joe Spiro, 38, graduated from high school and immediately went to work in New York's garment district. Beginning as a stock boy, Joe has slowly worked his way up the clothing industry ladder. His last job was at Cinderella Shoes, a manufacturer of fashionable yet affordable women's shoes. Mr. Spiro was Cinderella's top salesman for the last three years. Asked for a reference, Spiro's employer at Cinderella said he was "very sad" to see Mr. Spiro leave ("No great thinker, mind you, but he more than makes up for it in street smarts.") Mr. Spiro confesses to having no specific marketing experience, but claims that he "knows what the public wants."

How Much Will My Essay Affect My LSAT Score?

Not one bit.

Only three sections contribute to your LSAT score—Games, Arguments, and Reading Passages. An unmarked photocopy of your essay will be sent to the law schools to which you apply.

Who Will Read My Essay?

Possibly no one.

How well or poorly you do on the Writing Sample will almost certainly not affect your admissions chances.

Then Why Do Law Schools Require It?

Law schools feel guilty about not being interested in anything about you other than your grades and LSAT scores. Knowing that you have spent 30 minutes writing an essay for them makes them feel better about having no interest in reading what you have written.

If the Writing Sample Is So Unimportant, Why Discuss It?

The Writing Sample is the first thing you do when you take the LSAT. You want the first 30 minutes in the exam room to go smoothly. If you get stuck on the Writing Sample, you won't be in the proper frame of mind for the rest of the test. Spinning out a tight little essay is actually a good warm-up for the rest of the test—like stretching before a run.

There's also the possibility that a bored admissions officer will accidentally pass his eyes over what you have written. If your essay is ungrammatical, riddled with misspellings, off the topic, and wildly disorganized, the admissions officer may think somewhat less of you.

So we're going to assume that the writing sample counts a wee bit. You should assume the same thing, but don't lose sleep over it. No one ever got into law school because of the LSAT Writing Sample; no one ever got rejected because of it, either. Besides, good writing requires surprisingly few rules, and the rules we'll review will help your writing in general.

What Are They Looking For?

The general directions to the Writing Sample mention that law schools are interested in three things: essay organization, vocabulary, and writing mechanics. Presumably, writing mechanics covers grammar and style.

What They're *Really* Looking For

Researchers at the Educational Testing Service once did a study of essay-grading behavior. They wanted to find out what their graders really responded to when they marked papers, and which essay characteristics correlate most strongly with good scores.

The researchers discovered that the most important characteristic, other than "overall organization," is "essay length." Also highly correlated with good essay scores are number of paragraphs, average sentence length, and average word length. The bottom line? **Students who filled in all the lines, indented frequently, and used big words earned higher scores than students who didn't.**

We will discuss these points in more detail later. Since organization is the most important characteristic, let's start with that.

Essay Organization

Your essay should contain five paragraphs. In the first you state your opinion. In the last you restate your opinion. The three middle paragraphs form the body of your argument.

State your actual argument in three paragraphs. Three paragraphs demonstrate that your argument is concise as well as organized. Of course, if you find that one of your major ideas has secondary ideas, you may have to subdivide one of the middle paragraphs.

So your essay should consist of an introduction paragraph, a conclusion paragraph, and three main paragraphs for your argument. Five paragraphs total —rarely more, never fewer. The more you stick with a formula outline, the less thinking you'll have to do when you actually write.

What Are You Trying to Do?

You're trying to persuade your reader that one of two given alternatives is better. You cannot *prove* that one side is better; you can only make a case that it is. The test writers deliberately come up with boringly balanced alternatives so that you can argue for either one of them.

So choose a side and justify your choice.

Picking Sides

The directions stress that neither alternative is "correct." It doesn't matter which side you choose. Pick the alternative that gives you more to work with.

Another way to decide is to compile a little list of the pros and cons on your scratch paper. Then simply pick the alternative whose list of pros is longer. Let's see how you'd do this with the sample topic we've given you.

First, list each alternative (Spiro, Baldwin) as a heading. Underneath each heading draw two columns, one for the pros and one for the cons. Spend the first couple of minutes brainstorming the advantages and disadvantages of each choice. The key to brainstorming is *quantity,* not quality. You can select and discard points later.

Having brainstormed for pro and cons, select the ones you intend to keep and arrange them in order of importance, from *least* to *most* important.

For the purposes of this chapter, let's assume that we intend to give the nod to Spiro.

Don't Forget the Cons

Some students believe that if you're trying to make a case for something, you should bring up the advantages only. This is wrong.

To persuade readers (and your boss) that Mr. Spiro is the better choice, you must show that you have considered every argument that could be made for Ms. Baldwin, and found each one unconvincing.

Your argument, in other words, must show that you have weighed the pros and cons of *both* sides. The more forceful the objections you counter, the more compelling your position becomes.

Evaluating the Pros and Cons: The Criteria

As you think of pros and cons for each position, keep in mind the given criteria. Here you have two considerations—being innovative and being a team player. You must build your essay around these criteria, so don't ignore them. If your topic does not provide you with considerations, devise your own.

The criteria may not be compatible. If so, weigh the pros and cons in light of this situation. In our example, an innovative personality might not get along well with other people. You may want to rank the two criteria in terms of importance. Perhaps being an innovator is more important than being a team player. Perhaps not. Decide which consideration is more important. If you cannot decide, state so explicitly.

Can I Raise Other Issues?

You *must* weigh the two stated considerations, but nothing prevents you from introducing additional considerations.

We are told that Spiro and Baldwin have comparable salary requirements. But what about, say, expected raises and future promotions? A fast tracker may expect faster raises and promotions than someone who has not invested two years and $40,000 getting an MBA. And what about company loyalty. A fast tracker may not want to be held down to a single company for too long this early in her career. And what about knowledge of the industry versus knowledge of marketing?

You need not raise additional considerations, but if one occurs to you, and you have the time, mention it in passing. If none occurs to you, mention in the conclusion that you have evaluated the two options in view of the two stated considerations only, acknowledging that other considerations may be important.

Mr. Spiro Versus Ms. Baldwin: Brainstorming the Pros and Cons

Remember: Brainstorm first. Next, select the issues you intend to raise. Then rank the final issues, beginning with the least important.

To organize your brainstorming, use a rough chart like this one:

	INNOVATIVE?	TEAM PLAYER?	OTHER FACTORS
BALDWIN	possible; savvy marketer but knows nothing about industry	may not relate to garment workers	loyalty? expected promotions?
SPIRO	possible; street smarts; knows the market and industry	probably; having worked in industry for 20 years	loyalty? expected promotions?

Beginning Your Essay: Restating the Problem

Having brainstormed the pros and cons of each choice in light of the considerations, you are ready to start writing your essay.

Your first paragraph should do little more than produce your argument. Try not to use a tedious grade school opening like "The purpose of the essay I am about to write is to . . ." But if you can't think of a more interesting way to start, go ahead and be tedious. It won't matter.

There are several more interesting ways to introduce an argument. Which one you choose will influence how you organize the rest of your essay. Keep this in mind as you sketch your outline. We'll tell you more about this as we go along.

One possibility for an opening is simply to restate concisely the problem you are to address. Here's an example:

> Oh-So-Tight Jeans needs a Director of
> Marketing who is innovative and
> able to fit in with other employees.
> The two candidates are highly
> qualified, though in different ways.
> Since neither candidate is ideal, we must
> weigh their respective strengths and
> weaknesses in light of our corporate
> objectives.

This type of introduction sets up the conflict rather than immediately taking a side. The second, third, and fourth paragraphs are then devoted to weighing the specific advantages and disadvantages of each candidate. The author's preference isn't stated explicity until the final paragraph, although a clear case for one should emerge as the essay progresses.

An essay like this is really just an organized written version of the mental processes you went through in deciding which candidate to choose. In the first paragraph you say, in effect, "Here are the problems, the choices, and my decision." In the second, third, and fourth paragraphs you say, "Here are the pros and cons I weighed." In the fifth and final paragraph you say, "So you can see why I decided as I did."

Your hope is that the reader, by following your reasoning step-by-step, will decide the same thing. The great advantage of this kind of organization is that it *does* follow your mental processes. That makes it a natural and relatively easy method.

Beginning Your Essay: Putting Your Cards on the Table

It's also possible to write an essay in which you begin by announcing your decision. You state your preference in the first paragraph, back it up in the middle paragraphs, and then restate your preference with a concluding flourish in the final paragraph.

Here's an example of such an opening paragraph:

> Susan Baldwin is a young but highly accomplished marketing professional. As the youngest product manager at Natural Baby Foods, she gained a reputation as a savvy marketer. Her unquestionable marketing skills, however, may be overshadowed by her lack of familiarity with the garment business. Joe Spiro, by contrast, combines street smarts with over 20 years' experience in our industry. I believe that Mr. Spiro can more quickly familiarize himself with marketing than Ms. Baldwin can familiarize herself with our industry. For this, and other reasons, I believe that Mr. Spiro is our man, so to speak.

By introducing your argument in this way, you leave yourself with a great deal of latitude for handling the succeeding paragraphs. For example, you might use the second paragraph to discuss both candidates in light of the first consideration; the third paragraph to discuss both candidates in light of the second consideration; the fourth paragraph to weigh the considerations themselves; and the fifth and final paragraph to summarize your argument and restate your preference.

The Body of Your Argument

We've discussed the introductory and concluding paragraphs. Depending on your preference, and depending on the essay topic you actually confront, we recommend three variations for the middle paragraphs:

Variation I

Paragraph 2: Both sides in light of the first consideration
Paragraph 3: Both sides in light of the second consideration
Paragraph 4: Weighing the two considerations (and other considerations?)

Variation 2

    Paragraph 2:   Everything that can be said about Ms. Baldwin

    Paragraph 3:   Everything that can be said about Mr. Spiro

    Paragraph 4:   Why Mr. Spiro wins over Ms. Baldwin

Variation 3

    Paragraph 2:   A sentence or two for Ms. Baldwin, followed by three or four sentences for Mr. Spiro

    Paragraph 3:   A sentence or two for Ms. Baldwin, followed by three or four sentences for Mr. Spiro

    Paragraph 4:   A sentence or two for Ms. Baldwin, followed by three or four for Mr. Spiro

Again, if necessary you can divide any one of the three middle paragraphs into two paragraphs.

All three variations do the job. Choose a variation you feel comfortable with and memorize it. The less thinking you have to do on the actual exam, the better.

Transitions Between Issues

The basic order of positions is the other side first—briefly—then your side—at length. Since your essay will move back and forth between the two positions, your writing must inform the reader of the side you are discussing.

The English language contains a stock of formal words and phrases to do just that. The following list will give you the general idea of how to express the transition between positions:

To introduce the *other* side (Ms. Baldwin), use words or phrases like

    admittedly

    granted

    assuredly

    obviously

    of course

    undoubtedly

    to be sure

    unquestionably

    no doubt

    one cannot deny that

    nobody denies that

    one could argue that

    supporters for Ms. Baldwin might point out that

    we must acknowledge that

Then, to introduce *your* side (Mr. Spiro), use words to phrases like

notwithstanding
nevertheless
nonetheless
despite
yet
however
in spite of
although
still
in fact
even so
on the other hand

To emphasize your side, use words or phrases like

moreover
furthermore
indeed
in fact
what is more

Finally, to sum up your thesis, use words or phrases like

clearly
consequently
thus
therefore
in sum
we can see that

We're ready to consider the order of your points.

Last Impressions: Start with the *Other* Side

You may be wondering why we insist that you begin with the merits of the *other* side. Your motive for doing so is psychological—readers remember the last thing they read better than the first thing. You do not want to begin with your argument and then raise objections. Readers would then have the objections more firmly in mind than your position. If you give the good news first, readers will forget it when you tell them the bad news.

So raise any possible objections and dispense with them *before* getting to the merits of your position.

Start with Your *Weakest* Argument, Conclude with Your Strongest

You start with your weakest argument and build to your strongest argument for the same reason you begin by presenting the other side—readers will then finish your essay with your strongest argument most firmly in mind.

Vocabulary: It's Not What You Say but How You Say It

Students, fledgling writers, and even people who should know better confound the merely arcane with the profound. They believe, in other words, that smart people use difficult words and dumb people use simple words. Given a choice between a difficult word and a simple synonym, they will inevitably choose the heavyweight version. We believe that the precisely correct word should be used, simple or difficult.

Still, this prejudice against simple words is shared by enough people to justify the following compromise: Sprinkle your essay with a *few* ten-dollar words or phrases. Not too many, just enough to let readers know that you could turn on the juice and write like Henry James or Samuel Johnson whenever you want to.

Here's a list of sample words that will give you an idea of the sort we mean. If you aren't dead sure of the meaning of these or other words, look them up before you use them.

The Princeton Review Thesaurus of Pretty Impressive Words

The following list of words is not to be complete, nor is it in any particular order. Synonyms or related concepts are grouped where appropriate.

- example, instance, precedent, paradigm, archetype
- illustrate, demonstrate, highlight, acknowledge, exemplify, embody
- support, endorse, advocate, maintain, contend, espouse, champion
- supporter, proponent, advocate, adherent
- dispute, dismiss, outweigh, rebut, refute
- propose, advance, submit, marshal, adduce
- premise, principle, presumption, assumption, proposition
- advantages, merits, benefits
- inherent, intrinsic, pertinent
- indisputable, incontrovertible, inarguable, unassailable, irrefutable, undeniable, unimpeachable
- lame, unconvincing, inconclusive, dubious, specious
- compelling, cogent, persuasive
- empirical, hypothetical, theoretical

If you're feeling a little weak in the vocabulary department, today is as good a day as any to embark on a vocabulary campaign. Not that it's all that important for the LSAT. We recommend that all of our students improve their vocabulary. It is a proven fact that a person's vocabulary correlates directly with his or her success in life. We don't want to pass up this opportunity to plug another one of our books: *Word Smart*.

A Note on Diction

Make sure you don't spoil your display of verbal virtuosity by misusing or misspelling these or any other ten-dollar words. Also, get your idioms straight.

A final note on a common diction error. If, as in our Writing Sample, your choice involves only two options, *former* refers to the first and *latter* refers to the second. You cannot use these words to refer to more than two options.

Another common diction error occurs when comparing two or more things. The first option is *better* than the second, but it is not the *best*. No big deal.

Grammar

You are a big boy or girl now, so we will not insult your intelligence at this late point in your academic career with a grammar lesson. Instead we will give you a quiz to help you refresh yourself on the most common grammatical faux pas.

Our Comprehensive Grammar Quiz

<u>Directions:</u> The following ten questions illustrate the most common grammatical errors. Circle the error and rewrite the sentence. Some of the sentences may be correct. Answers are provided at the end of the chapter.

1. Although necessary only in minute quantities, the importance of trace minerals in human diets is now undeniable.

2. Exasperated beyond endurance, Mrs. Butterworth burst into tears over her husband singing in bed.

3. Our English teacher seems to be concerned not so much by content but instead by style.

4. Everyone at the starting line of the annual midnight marathon wore fluorescent numbers on their backs.

5. The doctor told her patient that she needed more rest and should take a long-overdue vacation.

6. An increasing number of scientists now believe that life may have begun as a crystalline form of clay.

7. The discrepancy between the theoretical and actual values is insignificant.

8. Karl Marx believed that social and political events merely reflect economical causes.

9. The recent decline in the dollar-yen exchange rate suggests that our economy is growing less rapidly than Japan.

10. For all its size, the elephant is a remarkably timid animal.

Style

Style is largely a personal matter. Write naturally. Do not adopt a tone you think will impress admissions committees.

Having said that, we conclude with a list of maxims. Violate them at your own risk.

Rules to Write By

1. Do not state things in the negative.
2. It is not a good idea to use pronouns.
3. Don't overuse contractions.
4. We feel/think/believe it's not a good idea to state your opinion vaguely.
5. The passive voice is to be avoided.

6. Avoid clichés like the plague.

7. Long sentences get more respect than short sentences.

8. Vary the length of your sentences. Often. Too many long sentences will numb your reader and invite grammatical errors.

9. Without being verbose, the more you write, the better. Look as if you took the assignment seriously. A big sea of white space at the end of your essay will stand out.

10. Don't be too cute, too funny, or too clever.

11. Write formally but naturally, without being pompous or ponderous.

12. Whereas the party of the first part (you) wants to be understood, the party of the second part (we) recommends that you avoid "law-yerese."

13. Indent your paragraphs clearly.

14. Strive for parallelism, it evidences an ordered mind as well as an ordered essay.

15. Put yourself in the appropriate frame of mind and write as if you were actually making the recommendation.

16. Do not assume that all the facts have been stated. Acknowledge assumptions briefly.

17. Avoid the past tense. Write in the present.

One Final Reminder

Write legibly! If you can't, *print* legibly!

A Sample Essay

> Oh-So-Tight Jeans is looking for a Director of Marketing and has narrowed its search to two candidates. The first, Susan Baldwin, graduated #1 in her Harvard Business School class three years ago. The second, Joe Spiro, has worked in the garment industry for 20 years. Oh-So-Tight is looking for someone who can deliver innovative campaigns while fitting in with the other employees. In view of these considerations, and since

salary requirements are similar, I must recommend Mr. Spiro over Ms. Baldwin.

The decision is a close call. Ms. Baldwin is unquestionably an excellent marketing professional. Although only 28, Ms. Baldwin's previous accounts at Natural Baby Foods earned her rapid promotion to product manager. Ms. Baldwin is well versed in all of the latest marketing techniques, and clearly knows how to use them. Unfortunately, Ms. Baldwin knows almost nothing about the garment industry. I do not think that we can wait for Ms. Baldwin to familiarize herself with our business. Marketing jeans is very different from marketing baby food. Moreover, I fear that the highly educated Ms. Baldwin is not the team player that we are looking for.

Mr. Spiro, on the other hand, combines street smarts with 20 years experience in our industry. It might be argued that Mr. Spiro is less educated than Ms. Baldwin, and we would agree. But what of it? Mr. Spiro has worked with people in the industry and undoubtedly knows quite a bit about our customers, having been a top-performing salesman for several years. As for his lack of formal marketing training, Mr. Spiro can always take a course or two at night school, if necessary. While we cannot be sure that Mr. Spiro is innovative, we cannot be sure that he is not. As for his being a team player, Mr. Spiro's 20 successful years in our industry testify to his getting along with garment center people.

In recommending Mr. Spiro, I have considered only the stated criteria of innovative ability and being a team player. I have assumed, further, that these criteria are equally important. I have ignored other considerations, although I think that these would further tip the balance in Mr. Spiro's favor. For example, I believe that Mr. Spiro will stay with Oh-So-Tight longer than Ms. Baldwin. Furthermore, I believe that Mr. Spiro is the more reasonable and realistic in terms of career advancement expectations.

In sum, both Ms. Baldwin and Mr. Spiro are highly qualified candidates. While Ms. Baldwin's deficiencies outweigh her strengths, Mr. Spiro's strengths outweigh his deficiencies. I recommend hiring him immediately.

Answers to our Grammar Quiz

1. Whenever a sentence begins with a phrase like *Although necessary only in minute quantities*, the subject modified by the phrase must follow immediately. Here the subject is *the importance* when it should be *trace minerals*. The sentence should read: *Although necessary only in minute quantities, trace minerals are undeniably important in human diets.*

2. Mrs. Butterworth is exasperated by her husband's singing, not by her husband. The sentence should read: *Exasperated beyond endurance, Mrs. Butterworth burst into tears over her husband's singing in bed.*

3. This sentence contains an incorrect idiom. It should read: *Our English teacher seems to be concerned not so much with content as with style.*

4. The subject of the sentence is *everyone*, a singular pronoun. The rest of the sentence must be consistent: *Everyone at the starting line of the annual midnight marathon wore a fluorescent number on his back.*

5. The word *she* is ambiguous. Is the doctor recommending that the patient go on a vacation or is she admitting that she herself should go on a vacation? *The doctor admitted to her patient that she . . .* , or *The doctor advised her patient that she . . .* would be correct.

6. This sentence contains a subtle redundancy. The word *believe* already suggests a probable truth. So the sentence should read: *An increasing number of scientists now believe that life began as a crystalline form of clay.* Incidentally, the subject of the sentence is *increasing number,* so the correct verb is the singular form *believe* (not believes).

7. Perfectly okay. The subject of the sentence is *discrepancy*. Since *discrepancy* is singular, the verb *(is)* should be singular. It is.

8. This sentence contains a diction error. *Economical* means "thrifty, affordable." The correct word is *economic.*

9. This sentence compares our economy with Japan, an equation that is not parallel. To compare our economy with the economy of Japan, the sentence should conclude: *. . . our economy is growing less rapidly than Japan's.*

10. *For all* is a standard idiom that means "notwithstanding" or "despite." This sentence is perfectly okay.

Summary

1. The Writing Sample is a thirty-minute ungraded essay whose topic is assigned. You will be asked to support either of two given positions.

2. Your essay will not affect your LSAT score.

3. In all likelihood, your essay will never be read.

4. The only reason for trying to do well on the Writing Sample is that doing so will put you in a good mood for the part of the test that counts.

5. What essay characteristics most impress readers? Essay length, number of paragraphs, average sentence length, and average word length.

6. The most important writing rules to remember are:

- fill in as much space as possible
- use a few pretty big words
- use a proper diction
- check your grammar and spelling
- indent your paragraphs clearly
- use precisely five paragraphs
- vary the length of your sentences
- don't get too cute, or too ponderous

7. It doesn't matter which alternative you choose. There is no "correct" answer.

8. Build your essay around the given considerations.

9. There are several possible ways to organize a solid, five-paragraph essay. Choose one that makes you feel comfortable. Prepare and memorize your organizational method before you go to take the test.

10. Mention all relevant pros and cons of both sides. Save the best for last.

CHAPTER 7

Taking the LSAT: Some Final Tips

Tick, Tick, Tick . . .

The LSAT is a week away. What should you do?

First of all, you should practice the techniques we have taught you on real LSATs. **Use only actual LSATs! Repeat after me: I will use only actual LSATs.** The practice tests in other LSAT preparation books won't help you; they aren't enough like real LSATs. Even the questions in this book are not as good as the real thing, although we have designed them according to the same statistical requirements used by the test writers.

If you don't have any real LSATs, your prelaw advisor may have a sample test or two. Ask your friends. If you have more than a couple of weeks, you can also order copies of LSATs directly from the LSAC/LSAS. For ordering information, see page 8.

Getting Psyched

The LSAT is a big deal, but don't let it intimidate you. Sometimes test takers become so nervous about doing well that they freeze on the test and murder their scores. Instead, think of the LSAT as a game. It's a game that you can become good at. The better you get, the less nervous you'll be. When you go into the test center, just think about all those poor people who will actually be trying to work out each and every question.

The best way to keep from getting nervous is to practice our techniques under simulated test conditions after you've mastered them. When you take the practice LSATs you've ordered from the LSAC/LSAS, *have someone else time you.* Take our word for it: Timing yourself is not the same thing.

Of course, taking the actual LSAT is much more nerve-racking than taking a practice test. Adrenaline somehow makes the time go by much faster. To simulate this time warp, you might want to allow yourself 25 to 30 minutes per section at home instead of the official 35 minutes.

It's all right to be nervous; the point of being prepared is to keep from panicking.

Should You Sleep for 12 Hours?

Some students have been told that they should get a lot of sleep the night before the LSAT. This probably isn't a good idea. If you aren't used to sleeping 12 hours a night, doing so will just make you groggy for the test. The same goes for going out and drinking a lot of beer: People with hangovers are not good test takers.

A much better idea is to get up early each morning for the entire week before the test and do practice questions as soon as you wake up. This will get your brain accustomed to functioning at that hour of the morning. You want to be sharp at test time.

Before you go to sleep the night before the test, spend an hour or so reviewing some of your previous practice tests. You don't want to exhaust yourself, but these reviews will help put you in the proper frame of mind for Saturday morning.

Closing Advice

Here are a few pointers for the test day and beyond:

1. You are supposed to take identification to your test center. Bring two official documents that have your name and photograph (driver's license, school ID, or current passport).

2. The only outside materials you are allowed to use on the test are No. 2 pencils and a wristwatch. *A wristwatch is an absolute necessity. Don't count on your proctor's being a reliable time keeper.* Digital watches are best; it's important to know whether you have a minute left, or 10 seconds. If you don't own one, borrow one. Proctors have been known to confiscate stopwatches and travel clocks. Technically, you should be permitted to use these, but you can never tell. Take a watch and avoid the hassles. (By the way, don't bring pencils that are too sharp. Sharp points break easily and take longer to fill in the answer sheet. Bring four slightly used pencils.)

3. Some proctors allow students to bring food into the test room; others don't. Take a soda and a candy bar with you and see what happens. If you don't flaunt them, they probably won't be confiscated. Save them until you're about halfway through the test. It takes about ten minutes for sugar to work its way to your tired brain. If the proctor yells at you, surrender your refreshments cheerfully and continue with the test.

4. Eat a normal breakfast that morning, but don't drink too much coffee or tea. You're going to be sitting in the same place for some four hours; you don't want to spend half your time running to the bathroom.

5. Make sure your desk isn't broken or unusually uncomfortable. If you are left-handed, ask for a left-handed desk. (The center may not have one, but it won't hurt to ask.) If the sun is in your eyes, ask if you can move. If the room is too dark, ask someone to turn on the lights. Don't hesitate to speak up. Some proctors just don't know what they're doing.

6. During the test, don't spend a lot of time darkening in your responses. You will see some test takers trancelike, aesthetically darkening in every last white space before going to the next question. Darken the response, then move on. Remember to circle your answers in your booklet and to transfer them to your answer sheet in groups.

7. During the breaks, get up and stretch. Clear your head. Some proctors forget to give breaks, so you might want to remind the proctor before the test begins by asking when you will get your first break.

8. You can cancel your score, but a notice that you've taken the test will appear on your record. Since the LSAC/LSAS averages all the LSATs you've taken, cancel your score if you know you bombed. The key word is *know.* Don't cancel your score because you have a bad feeling—students frequently have an exaggerated sense of how many mistakes they made, and it's possible you did much better than you fear. When you *know* you've done poorly, and you have another opportunity to take the LSAT, cancel your score and gear up for the next time around.

9. About a month after the test, you will receive a sample test booklet along with your answer sheet. If you plan to retake the LSAT, we recommend that before you look at the answers, you do this test again. Compare your responses here with your actual exam room responses. Were they different? Did you repeat your mistakes? Doing this test again will let you see how many of your mistakes were attributable to the willies on exam day, how many were

attributable to time pressure, and how many were attributable to just plain ignorance.

If you're not planning to retake the LSAT, give your booklet to another prelaw student so that he or she can start preparing.

CHAPTER 8

About The Princeton Review LSAT Course

The Princeton Review was founded in New York City in 1981 to prepare students for the SAT. Our SAT students improved their scores an average of 150 points, so in a few years we became the largest SAT course in the country. In 1985 we started our courses for the graduate exams.

Our LSAT course consists of between 40 and 50 hours of classroom instruction. To ensure plenty of individual attention, class size is strictly limited—never more than 15 students. Moreover, classes are arranged according to ability, so your fellow students will be at the same level of achievement. At least once a week, smaller workshops meet to provide an even more thorough review. If you want still more practice, you can arrange for private tutoring *at no additional cost.* (By the way, in addition to our LSAT course, The Princeton Review also offers private tutoring.)

Each student is assigned to a class on the basis of his or her score on the first of our four diagnostic LSATs. These diagnostic tests are actual LSATs to give students accurate feedback about their performance and improvement. Within a few days of each test, we'll provide you with a detailed computerized analysis of your responses. This personalized assessment will pinpoint your test-taking strengths and weaknesses. Armed with this evaluation, you and your instructor will be able to study with maximum efficiency. For example, you'll be able to say to yourself, "On the reading passages I do well on the theme questions but I need to concentrate more on the inferential questions."

All the practice tests used by the Princeton Review are actual LSATs. The materials you will use throughout the course have been prepared by our research staff to reflect the most up-to-date techniques we have developed to crack the LSAT. For example, when the LSAC/LSAS contracted with new test developers in 1986, Princeton Review students were prepared for the subtle changes in test design. When the LSAT changed again this year, Princeton Review students were prepared well in advance.

If you'd like more information about The Princeton Review and its courses, you can reach us at our toll-free number, (800) 333-0369, or call the office nearest you.

Princeton Review Offices Near You

Since new Princeton Review sites are opening almost monthly, you might want to call our toll-free number to see if a new site has opened since the publication of this book.

Arizona
All locations — 602/952-8850

California
Orange County (Anaheim area) — 714/553-9411
Los Angeles area — 213/474-0909
Sacramento area — 916/447-4255
San Diego area — 619/695-9952
San Jose area (Silicon Valley) — 408/268-9674
San Francisco & Marin County — 415/891-9977

Colorado
All locations — 303/428-8000

Connecticut
Hartford area — 203/651-3557
All others — 203/775-4642

District of Columbia
All locations — 202/797-1410

Florida
Miami — 305/445-3933
Orlando — 407/831-2400

Georgia
All locations — 404/233-0980

Illinois
Chicago area — 312/880-2412

Kansas
All locations — 913/469-8388

Louisiana
All locations — 404/233-0980

Maine
All locations — 603/433-7090

Maryland
Baltimore — 301/332-0891
All others — 202/797-1410

Massachusetts
Amherst area — 413/584-6849
Boston area — 617/277-5280

Michigan
All locations — 313/851-1133

Minnesota
All locations   612/379-3937

Missouri
St. Louis area   314/567-3787
Kansas City area   913/469-8388

New Hampshire
All locations   603/433-7090

New Jersey
Camden area   215/923-2077
All other locations   609/683-0082

New York
New York City   212/874-7600
                                                718/935-0091
Long Island   516/925-2999
Westchester & Rockland   203/775-4642

Upstate
Albany area   518/458-8552
Binghamton area   607/773-0311
Putnam & Duchess   914/997-1311
Syracuse area   315/476-8378

North Carolina
Chapel Hill area   919/967-7209
Charlotte area   704/334-1482

Ohio
Cleveland area   216/360-0100
Columbus area   614/794-1035

Pennsylvania
Philadelphia area   215/923-2077
Pittsburgh area   413/362-1052

Puerto Rico
All locations   809/268-2135

Rhode Island
All locations   401/861-5080

Texas
Austin area   512/474-8378
Dallas area   214/890-0099
Fort Worth area   817/335-4160
Houston area   713/688-5500
San Antonio area   512/341-1942

Vermont
All locations   802/658-6653

Virginia
All locations   202/797-1410

Washington (State)
All locations   206/325-1341

INTERNATIONAL SITES
Hong Kong   011-852-5-598-045

Japan
Tokyo   011-813-446-8985

Pakistan
Lahore   011-92-42-872-315

Spain
Madrid   011-341-446-5541

ALL OTHER LOCATIONS   800/333-0369

About the Author

Adam Robinson was born in 1955. He graduated from the Wharton School at the University of Pennsylvania before earning a law degree at Oxford University in England. Robinson, a rated chess master, devised and perfected the now-famous "Joe Bloggs" approach to beating standardized tests in 1980, as well as numerous other core Princeton Review techniques. A free-lance author of many books, Robinson has collaborated with The Princeton Review to develop a number of its courses. He lives in New York City.

The Princeton Review Library

Take the pain and strain out of getting into the school of your choice with the smartest prep books for standardized tests. Whether you are aiming for undergraduate or graduate school, The Princeton Review has a book for you.

Going to college? The Princeton Review Library includes three outstanding books to help you get into the school of your choice.

The Princeton Review—
Cracking the System
The SAT® and PSAT®—1992
Edition by John Katzman and
Adam Robinson
Test Guide, 304 pages,
8⅜ x 10⅞, charts and graphs,
$13.00 paper (Canada $17.50)
ISBN 0-679-73486-4

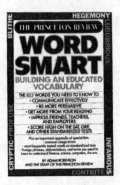

The Princeton Review—Word
Smart: Building an
Educated Vocabulary
Education, 256 pages, 6 x 9,
$7.95 paper (Canada $9.95)
ISBN 0-394-75686-X

The Princeton Review—
Cracking the System:
College Admissions
Reference, 192 pages, 6 x 9,
$7.95 paper (Canada $9.95)
ISBN 0-394-75189-2

If you're going to graduate, business or law school, don't let rusty test-taking skills get in the way. The Princeton Review Library offers three excellent books.

The Princeton Review—
Cracking the System:
The GRE®—1992 Edition
Test Guide, 304 pages,
8⅜ x 10⅞, $13.00 paper
(Canada $17.50)
ISBN 0-679-73487-2

The Princeton Review—
Cracking the System:
The GMAT®—1992 Edition
Test guide, 240 pages,
8⅜ x 10⅞, charts and graphs,
$13.00 paper (Canada $17.50)
ISBN 0-679-73367-1

The Princeton Review—
Cracking the System:
The LSAT®—1992 Edition
Test Guide, 176 pages,
8⅜ x 10⅞, line drawings,
$13.00 paper (Canada $17.50)
ISBN 0-679-73488-0